What Were You Thinking

Some Common Thinking Errors and What to Do About Them

By Joseph Bennette

ISBN 1440465622

EAN-13 9781440465628

Ideas, suggestions, recommendations, and issues presented in this book are for consideration only and are not to take the place of competent medical or psychological assistance. Client stories in this book are true; the names and identifiable details have been changed to protect client confidentiality.

Compassion, imagination, wonder and rational thought are among the greatest human attributes. It seems to me there's no better time than now to exhibit them!

Dedication

This book explores my journey of discovery into my own thinking errors. Most of my journey I've traveled with my sweetheart, companion, wife, and best friend, Carol. She inspires me and challenges me to think outside convention. To her I dedicate this book and my life.

Acknowledgements

- John Phillips, who crafted the draft version of *10 Cognitive Thinking Errors* from the work of Aaron Beck and others, in *Feeling Good: The New Mood Therapy*, by David Burns.

- Jonathan Altfeld and Kenrick Cleveland, who so freely shared their insights into and expertise in Neuro-Linguistics and human nature with me.

- The all-powerful fuehrer of the online email list, Mindlist, Elroy Carter, whose clear-headed thinking and exemplary use of the Meta Model helped me immensely. So many members of that email group have helped me develop my particular views on useful and effective ways to think – and were willing to point out some of my own errors in thinking. I can't thank them enough.

- Carol Bennette, whose insights and sometimes odd yet useful ways of viewing life gave rise to this book.

Fundamental Thinking Error #1

"I know."

Fundamental Thinking Error #2

"I'm right."

Together they make Fundamental Thinking Error #3

"I know I'm right."

Contents

Some Common Thinking Errors and What to Do About Them

Some Common Thinking Errors and What to Do About Them

It is easier to get older than it is to get wiser.

Some Common Thinking Errors and What to Do About Them

Introduction

Thinking Errors

Just what are thinking errors? Is it a thinking error to disbelieve what someone else believes? Is it a thinking error to misjudge someone's character? Is it a thinking error to challenge convention? Just what do I mean when I subtitle my book, "Some Common Thinking Errors and What to Do About Them"?

We're thinking all the time. Some of that thinking tends to bring about outcomes that differ from our intentions or wishes. Frustration is often the result when outcome doesn't match intention or expectation. Maybe you're seeking to lose a few pounds and have discovered that wishing isn't enough. Maybe you've tried diets and other programs to lose some weight yet always find yourself defeated when you regain the pounds later. There is probably a thinking error at the root. Fix the thinking error and amazingly, the pounds drop like rain.

Every living creature makes mistakes. By "mistakes" I mean choices resulting in disappointment, frustration, missteps, danger, and death rather than the intended or expected outcome. Humans are no exception. We make mistakes – loads of them!

We will continue to make mistakes. That is the course of life. The intent of this book is to help you perhaps lessen the number of mistakes and make your wishes come true more often in the way you wish them to come true.

I don't intend to tell you the truth about life or to support any belief or belief system; only to investigate and challenge some common thinking errors. If you find after clearing these thinking errors that you are more supported in your beliefs, great! My hope is that you will find the courage to challenge your thinking and investigate your beliefs with clear thinking processes. I hope you will find the courage to change your life as necessary.

Changing My Religion

I was with a client one Friday in 1999 when the door to my small session room burst open. It was our receptionist. "Emergency call for you on line one." Emergency? I don't like the sounds of the word "emergency". "Please take a number and I'll call them back in a moment." I finished up with my client who was at a crucial juncture.

"It's Jan," I recognized my Dad's wife's voice through her tears when I finally got to the phone and returned the call. "Your dad has had a heart attack. He's in the hospital. It's serious. Can you drive over?"

My Dad was a "hometown boy" – born and raised in the very same town. Now, it appeared, he was going to die in that same town. I raced the thirty plus miles to be with my dad, praying fervently for his recovery as thirty miles felt like five hundred.

When I arrived, my dad was comatose, hoses and wires connected to every pore it seemed. I posted vigil with him into the night and at last, life support could no longer sustain him and I watched in helpless despair as they disconnected him according to his written wishes. The medical crew left us.

We were alone. It was an aloneness I'd never felt before. Deep and sudden.

I cradled my dad's head in my arms as I felt whatever life there was in him fade completely away, leaving me with a cold, lifeless mass of flesh for a companion.

As a religious person, I was sure I'd "feel his passing" – but I didn't. There was nothing at all. No "spiritual" manifestations or anything. Just a cold, hard, fact – he was dead. And that, it seemed, was that.

I'd never felt so vulnerable to the grim reaper. It was as though God had removed my protective shield and exposed me to the harsh inevitability of death. No longer would my father run ahead of me keeping death at bay – a strange thought, I know, but it was how I felt at the time.

For the next three days I cried a lake-full of tears. I mulled every nuance of our relationship in my mind – releasing deeply held resent-

Some Common Thinking Errors and What to Do About Them

ments, regrets, attachments, neediness, "shoulds", and missed opportunities. With my sobs I washed away all the future years of getting to know my Dad as an elderly man. I was surprised by the depth of emotions I held for him.

I also cried tears of joy for the years I got to enjoy him. He wasn't a great statesman or a well-known celebrity. He was "just another" human being who was born, lived out his life, and died. But for reasons I still don't fully understand, his life had particular significance for me. He was my dad. That was enough.

A Rude Awakening!

That awful weekend in 1999 shook me to my core. It caused me to reach deep down into my mind's private places – into places I don't like to frequent. I visited my doubts. I really wanted to have it out with God for taking my Dad so young. I wasn't happy with Him. I wanted ANSWERS!

I rationalized that God had taken my Dad because He had some purpose in mind that I didn't understand. I prayed that I'd understand that purpose. I asked my church leaders for assistance – my mind was suddenly awash with questions now that the emotional storm had subsided.

When Dad passed away, there was no "spiritual wind" or "fluttering wings of angels" or "warmth of the spirit" or anything. There was just a lifeless, limp corpse. I was very disappointed that even though I really wanted to believe in spiritual things, nothing happened at all – Dad's body ceased functioning and it died. The consciousness I knew as my Dad was simply gone. I figured it was some kind of spiritual test. I was determined to keep God in His supreme place – and not give in to what was becoming more and more obvious.

My religious leaders had lots of answers for me. It's just that for every answer they gave me, I had a question – "could there be some other equally good answer?" And my answer was always, "Yes! There is!" I was now awash in ANSWERS!

One answer kept nagging at me, though. Maybe Dad had simply died like all other animals die. And when he died, his "spirit" ceased just like his body. I was faced with absolutely no evidence for or against his hav-

Some Common Thinking Errors and What to Do About Them

ing a spirit. The only "evidence" I had was what others had told me. I suddenly realized that the only "confirmation" of spirit was that which I manufactured for myself. If I didn't sustain the belief in a spirit, I could just as easily interpret the evidence I experienced in a totally natural, non-spiritual way.

I had two competing theories – Spiritual, in which Dad's spirit continued in some afterlife; or Natural, in which Dad's consciousness died with his body. I knew which theory I WANTED to believe! But WANTING something to be true does not make it so.

That realization put me on to questioning my deepest beliefs – and questioning my way of thinking. I recalled a time thirty years earlier when I was investigating my Christian church that one missionary suggested that I should "want to believe" – and that I'd then discover the truth. I wondered how many of my "truths" were true because I WANTED them to be true. I was primed to challenge Fundamental Thinking Error #1 – "I know."

The most common lie is that which one lies to himself; lying to others is relatively an exception. - Friedrich Nietzsche

I wondered if I was sustaining a religious belief with presuppositions I could no longer support – presuppositions based on the trust I had given certain human authorities. When I traced back my presuppositions – those concepts upon which one builds subsequent beliefs without question – those things we "suppose" without further proof – I had to acknowledge that all my religious beliefs were based on unsupportable notions of the nature of the universe. Those notions came to me from *people* purporting to speak for God.

That realization put me into a new frame of mind – one in which I had to admit that I really *didn't know* whether or not I was right. I was primed to challenge Fundamental Thinking Error #2 – "I'm right."

I realized that the religious theory I'd believed was true might not be true. I entertained for the first time since High School the possibility of another answer to the "Big Questions." I wondered for the first time if I wasn't the victim of faulty thinking – what my son-in-law calls "Stinkin' Thinkin'."

I questioned whether my religious certainty was a sign of my arrogance rather than a testimony of the knowledge of truth. I began to wonder about my answers. I was becoming interested in questions again.

It was time for me to challenge Fundamental Thinking Error #3: "I know I'm right."

The Pall of Certitude vs the Freedom of Doubt

The only appropriate attitude for man to have about the big questions is not the arrogant certitude that is the hallmark of religion - but doubt. Doubt is humble and that is what man needs to be - because human history is a litany of getting shit dead wrong. – Bill Maher, Religulous

Life is, by nature, ambiguous. Perhaps we *should* doubt certainty. Perhaps we *should* doubt our answers. Perhaps we *should* question everything! Now there's some shoulds for you!

As a past member of a Christian sect, I know the appeal that answers and certainty have on the human mind. Religions offer answers intended to satisfy our deepest fears – fears of death and oblivion, fears of being alone, but mostly fears of the unknown – as well as our deepest wishes and hopes.

When we're faced with the unknown, our fear of it makes us want answers like we want air when we're under water. My survival instincts dictate that I escape death by whatever means – even if that means is illusory. The ultimate unknown – that which is beyond death – scared me more than death itself.

I also had hopes – hopes of a sweet life beyond this one. My native curiosity makes me want to know what will happen as time passes beyond my lifetime. I want to see how my children and grandchildren do over time. I want to see my great-great-great-grandchildren. I had hoped to enjoy sweet peace and the light of infinite intelligence. I had deep hopes.

As a religious person, I already had answers that satisfied my fears and hopes. The problem was...

Answers are not necessarily equivalent with truth.

Truth is that which is – independent of belief, agreement, or acceptance. For years, I thought I KNEW the truth – Fundamental Thinking

Error #1 - and based on my knowledge, I wasn't afraid to tell others – with confidence - Fundamental Thinking Error #2. The certainty of my beliefs gave me assurance and security. It also made me judgmental and fueled my ego and prejudices. It feels good to be right, you know!

> Lesson learned: Errors can occur when *thinking* is confused with *feeling*. *Feeling* good about something does not make that something true.

What if... I'm wrong!

My mind kept asking, "what if?" – "What if I DON'T know the truth?" What if I just THINK I know the truth? What if I'm making something true by WANTING it to be true? What if my fear is driving my thinking? What if... I've been wrong!

I was *feeling* insecure while *thinking* about uncertainties. As long as I resisted the urge to satisfy my fear, I was free to investigate my questions without .

I came to appreciate that not being certain can be an interesting place to be – because uncertainty opens the door to other possibilities. It's also a very scary place to be – because you have no assurances, no security, and no certainty. And what if I were to come to discover that the truths I held so certainly were not truths at all?

To recap:

Certitude → Security → Safety

Uncertainty → Insecurity → Freedom

In my religion, doubt was thought of as the Devil's tool for prying one away from "the Truth" – meaning away from the church. I ran the serious risk of being damned forever! According to my "truth", I was facing a fate worse than death – eternal damnation – just for asking a question.

In practice, however, my doubts simply took me away from certitude. What I discovered was that doubt was my key to the mysteries beyond my fears and hopes. As I soon learned...

Doubt was completely liberating!

Some Common Thinking Errors and What to Do About Them

For the first time in my life I considered that maybe there is no God, no Heaven, no Hell. I contemplated what it would be like to be without a religion. Would I fall into despair because my fears were now exposed and I'm no longer safe from death, oblivion, aloneness, and the unknown? Would I feel hopeless as my eternal hopes disappeared? Perhaps I could feel that way. Instead, I…

Rejoiced!

Suddenly I realized how important my life is to me! If there is no life after death for me to "make up" or "repent" or regret or watch or take up the harp or do anything else, then all of my life must be right NOW. Consciousness is extremely precious when viewed in this light – when it's gone, it's gone forever – so make the most of it while you have it! Each life on earth takes on much more value for me because I appreciate its fleeting nature.

I'm all for religions as they fill a need for many. To the end they help people realize happiness and a sense of joy, and help them make the most of their lives, giving them a sense of purpose, regulating societal norms for the betterment of all, and reminding people of their responsibilities to one another, they have their place.

Perhaps in the future we will "get it" that we have only enough time in our short lifetimes for joy and happiness. With no time for greed, avarice, jealousy, hopelessness, and ignorance, the seven deadly sins might be viewed as sins against time rather than sins against God. Perhaps we'll come to realize the power of our minds to create peace and harmony amongst ourselves and our fellow beings on this planet. Maybe we'll even extend that peace to other planets, who knows?

My Intention

This book is an attempt to share my journey of self discovery by way of short articles, stories, and quotes that have helped me accept the truth – that I really don't know anything for sure - that doubt and an inquiring mind are two of humanity's most valuable assets.

Please keep in mind as you read that I'm not presenting truth. Rather, I'm presenting ideas that have been useful to me and to others. By useful,

Some Common Thinking Errors and What to Do About Them

I mean that which served to move my thoughts away from ancient superstitious beliefs and toward rational, compassionate thinking.

As we evolve as a specie, may we make the virtues of honesty, appreciation, respect, genuine affection, and reason our evolutionary goals. We owe no less to our descendants and to the planet that sustains us.

Evolution

I wonder if evolution as Darwin envisioned it is a central underlying precept of our universe. Things tend to start small and evolve into ever larger, more complex systems that then adapt to their environments. Gravity causes smaller bodies to combine into larger ones, for example.

Inherent in evolution is the principle of adaptation to environment. In living systems, organisms tend to either adapt to their environments or die. In the ethereal, ideas also tend to either adapt to their environment or die. Even cosmologically, planetary systems tend to either adapt or die or leave for a different environment in which they can survive.

Human societies and even my own body are constantly in a process of adaptation to environment. Successful adaptation is the name of the survival game.

As you consider the ideas put forth in this book, those ideas will swim in your mind and thoughts. I hope they will strengthen your mental and emotional environment. This book is the result of my mental and emotional evolution.

I have arranged this book as a collection of thoughts rather than as a cohesive or orderly narrative. I figure the order will work itself out in the mind of the reader. I've included a table of contents for your convenience.

It is not my job to think for you. My intent is to simply point out ways in which you might "re-adapt" on your evolutionary path.

I dedicate this book to the human attributes of compassion and rational thought. I hope we will exhibit them soon.

Enough about me. Let's talk about US.

Some Common Thinking Errors and What to Do About Them

The Cosmic Zoo

"Extraterrestrial intelligent life may be almost ubiquitous. The apparent failure of such life to interact with us may be understood in terms of the hypothesis that they have set us aside as part of a wilderness area or zoo."[1]

I like this hypothesis – I think perhaps it puts humans into cosmological perspective.

When we realize that we are insignificant in the cosmological, geological, and time realms, perhaps we can begin to come to grips with just who we really are.

There are those who believe we are "created in the image of God" – although it seems more likely to me that god is created by man in his (man's) own image in an attempt to create a false sense of importance (we like feeling important, you know). This "Child of God" perspective seeks to implant humanity at the pinnacle of importance cosmologically – as "children of God" we are more important than all the trillions of stars, billions of galaxies, millions of galaxy clusters, and the infinite space we call the universe – as well as countless life forms yet to be discovered by us (refer to opening quote).

My point is that we NEED to feel important when we are actually infinitesimally unimportant (in the cosmological sense). As such, perhaps we are willing to "bend" the truth to suit our needs – that is, perhaps we are willing to lie to comfort ourselves. To further the illusion of importance, we'll even squabble amongst ourselves and jockey for positions of power and influence in our societies – the insignificant seeking to dominate the insignificant. We believe someone is important if they are rich or famous or strong or beautiful or…

But what if one day something or someone from "out there" were to suddenly take an interest in the "zoo" and come visiting? What if they had the power to suddenly and permanently irradiate life from our measly little planet (think BIG object – like a planetoid)? What then? How important would our world leaders, ultra-rich, or influential, famous people be in comparison to such a global threat?

We are so powerless we can't even move an object the size of Los Angeles from an intercept course with Earth even if we were to discover it years ahead of impact. We can't even exist on another planet without life-support equipment – and then only for a VERY short time. If such an object were to put us in the cross-hairs, we'd realize just how insignificant and powerless we really are...

Can you teach a dog nuclear physics? Can we comprehend the truth? I wonder.

We measure distance in earthly units of miles or kilometers when we live in a neighborhood where the nearest sister planet is millions of such miles away; and in which the nearest solar neighbor is billions of billions of miles away – so far we measure the distances in time (a light year is the distance light travels in a full earth year). We live only an instant in geological terms. And less than that in cosmological terms.

Cosmic joke number one: We think we are so intelligent that we seek out "other" intelligent life – in hopes we might communicate with them.

How significant are we really? I wonder.

We are, I suppose, an interesting species. We emote. We envision. We care. We lie. We cheat. We betray. We laugh. We grieve. We wonder. We explore. We are infinitely curious. I wonder if rather than what we are, it is what we imagine that makes us significant at all.

How significant do you think imagination is in the cosmos? I wonder.

Imagination is a doorway into another dimension. When you cross the threshold of imagination into another dimension of thought, you transcend the zoo – as there are no limits to imagination. In this one aspect we can envision and embrace the whole of all that is. We can expand our consciousness beyond the confines of the zoo. We can join the observers if we choose to do so.

We can choose to embrace our insignificance by giving up our need for importance and start now to treat each other with respect, choosing the way of peace, appreciation, harmony, and love.

Biocentrism

Although highly technical and highly controversial, a "new" theory of everything concludes that "the universe is created by life and not the other way around." (Lanza, 2009)[2]

If Lanza's theory holds true (we'll probably never know because his theory is as impossible to prove or disprove as is String Theory – just makes a whole lot more sense considering the evidence), then what you think and believe really does have a significant impact on hard reality.

In a nutshell, according to biocentrism, time (and space) does not exist independently of the life that notices it. This is particularly evident in the physics of the infinitesimally small (quantum mechanics) in which subatomic particles seem to be everywhere at once unless observed, in which case they suddenly appear in only one place at one time.

The Illusion of Will

"We like to think of our decisions as willful acts, but that may be an illusion. Many decisions may be much more directly and automatically driven by what our brain is sensing." (Corbetta, 2009)[3]

Mark Twain, in his essay "What Is Man?" argues that humans do not command their minds or the opinions they form. "You did not form that [opinion]," a speaker identified as "old man" says in the essay. "Your [mental] machinery did it for you – automatically and instantly, without reflection or the need of it."

I hear a lot about "free will" and I often wonder just how "free" it is. Further, I wonder, when you make a choice, how much of your "higher" mental faculty was involved in its making compared to how much animal instinct was involved? I suggest that most of the time our animal brain is in charge – and that choices made are made based on the "basest" part of us – the part we call the animal part.

I know we don't like to hear that we are "no better than the beast" but, hey – if the shoe fits…

When you come to understand and appreciate your animal side, you can harness it for useful work – just as you would a horse or mule. Knowing the language of animals helps, too, in communicating effectively with this part of yourself. Your animal self is essential to your survival – you NEED it. It's just that you don't have to be in its service yourself – you can direct it as you would if you were the rider on a horse.

Let me reiterate – you are an animal – a life form within the environment we call earth – get used to the idea – it's most likely the truth. Unique among animals on earth, humans can think in abstractions, appreciate the intricacies and mysteries of physics and chemistry, explore beyond earthly environs, appreciate creativity and art, and possess the ability to destroy all life on the planet – or extend it beyond earth.

Our choices are already made – by our animal selves – that thinks in terms of threat vs. benefit and pleasure vs. pain. There is thought beyond these parameters – to get there, however, requires one to transcend the need for survival. And that's where it gets tricky – because to explore beyond threat vs. benefit and pleasure vs. pain might require one to put at risk all they treasure in life – including life itself – and likely lose it in the process (thus the risk).

I suggest we embrace our animal selves – that we honor it and embrace it as we would a treasured pet – rather than believing that our animal self (based on threat/benefit, pleasure/pain) is our higher self. What would happen if we were to put our rational, logical, higher mental orders to work doing more than the simple chore of seeing to the mental and emotional survival needs and desires of our animal selves?

What is beyond money and power? Influence and attraction? Fear and doubt? Addiction? Compulsion? Greed, control, pride, envy, and lust? What is beyond threat/benefit and pleasure/pain? What is the next step in human evolution if not that which is beyond mere survival of the species?

When man stepped onto the surface of the moon for the first time, we extended our life form onto another celestial body – what will that mean for the universe beyond? THAT will be a choice I hope we'll make using our higher mind rather than our animal minds.

Some Common Thinking Errors and What to Do About Them

Chapter 1

How We Think Makes a Difference

Seven Stages of Projection to Celebration

Sometimes we get caught up in the blame game. We are so sure that it is someone else's fault that we are poor, or angry, or left out, or disrespected, or unappreciated, or ugly, or fat, or clumsy, or afraid - we are the victim of somebody else's bad behavior. Because we are the victim of somebody else's actions, someone else's mistakes, we are helpless to change our circumstance and must take what comes our way. Blaming makes us feel better temporarily, but somehow, blaming others never really satisfies us for long because blaming others never brings about a change of condition. After a while, we grow accustomed and maybe even addicted to the blame game.

The law is that you can only change that which you own. So long as you give your power for change to another through blame, you are powerless to effect change. You will continue to be the victim of others to whom you have given your power. That's the law of the universe.

If you are unhappy and it is the fault of someone else that you are unhappy, you are in a power-less position. You must rely upon the other person for a change of heart – a change that may never happen. Why leave your happiness up to someone else when you can account for it yourself? Why leave yourself in a powerless position when you can reclaim your power and make your life as you please? Would you like to be happy in your life? Would you like to be free of guilt, shame, anger, frustration, and disappointment?

You can change your life substantially by taking personal responsibility for yourself. This is called personal accountability. You account for yourself. You are doing this already, yet may not be aware.

Becoming aware is the secret to enjoying a life of wonderful abundance, glorious happiness, and blissful success. And it occurs in seven stages.

Stage 1. I Project Myself Onto Others.

I acknowledge my own leadership, beauty, wisdom, anger, etc., by expressing or seeing it in and through others. "They" are beautiful. "They" are angry. "They" are making me unhappy. This is the stage of expectation and blame. It is also the stage of justification and rationalization in which I reason that it is not my fault that I feel as I do – it is "their" fault, because... I project my feelings out and away from myself because I'm afraid to own them myself - afraid they will hurt too much. Expecting someone else to own my feelings can be frustrating and stressful and so my world is filled with stress, dissatisfaction, and disappointment. In this stage it can be a challenge to see myself for who I really am because I am so busy needing THEM to fulfill MY expectations – needing THEM to make ME happy. And because THEY cannot possibly always fulfill MY expectations, I am often unhappy. And it's THEIR FAULT.

Stage 2. My Projection Fades.

The OTHER person fails to fulfill MY expectations of them by acting in a different way than I expected them to act. Maybe my idol has fallen from grace or my angry neighbor does me a kind act. This is the stage of excuses. When I see my projection of others fading I recover my images through rationalizing or creating excuses and reasons for their behaviors, looks, attitudes, etc., thinking or explaining that "everyone has a hard day from time to time" or "even a bad apple can have a good side." In this stage I can justify my fading projections, restoring them to their place. This stage usually results in my return to stage one. I can loop between stage one and two for a lifetime. OR, I can become aware of my condition and move on to the next stage.

Stage 3. My Projection Disintegrates.

The one I have projected myself upon completely blows my image of them and cannot regain it. My idol confesses to some hideous crime, or my neighbor turns out to be a nice guy after all. I am then faced with the awful reality of my self-imposed deception; I immediately begin to express disappointment, anger, and then blame. This is the stage of choice. I may revert to stage one, finding someone else to hold my projection, or I may move on to stage 4. My projection may be important enough to me that I will repeat these first three stages for years – maybe a lifetime.

Stage 4. Taking Account.

Some Common Thinking Errors and What to Do About Them

I recognize the projection and see it for the fantasy that it is. There is an element of grief at this point; grief for the hurt I have unconsciously inflicted upon others. I begin to act responsibly by consciously cleaning up the messes I created in my unconscious stages of projection. This is the stage of honesty as I accept the possibility of seeing in a new way. In this stage I take responsibility for my own creative thought processes and choose consciously to redirect my thoughts. In this stage, I may gain a glimpse of the real me. This is the stage of calamity. Because I am taking accountability for myself and my behaviors and feelings, it would take a calamitous event to shake me back to stage one where I can once again blame and project. Parts of me want to return to the familiar environment of the blame game and so I may set myself up for a calamity in which I can blame someone else – or a group of others – for the terrible thing that happens to me or to someone I care about. If I revert to blame, I will return to stage one. With awareness, I can move on to the next stage.

Stage 5. Expressing Compassion.

In the process of grieving, the recovery of self begins. I express compassion for myself by honoring the individuality and uniqueness of my thoughts and those of others. In this stage, I start out fresh with self-esteem through forgiveness and taking a deeper look at what my perceptions are or have been. By doing this I choose new, ever more productive methods for imaging my world. Judgment is replaced by compassion - I acknowledge others as worthy of my esteem regardless of their actions. That is because I am beginning to accept my own worthiness. This is the stage of listening. I now hear past the words and actions or behaviors of others into the realm of understanding and empathy.

Stage 6. Appreciation.

I begin to recognize in this stage that all I perceive in others is only what I have projected from within me. In this stage I gratefully regain the power I've given away to others; power to write my own script; power to change my script; power of my own innate personhood. I accept and feel gratitude for the mirror that life is to me. Blame is replaced by acceptance and appreciation. I respect the rights of others to be and act as they do because I accept that "they" are just mirrors of me. Life at this stage is

Some Common Thinking Errors and What to Do About Them

enjoyed as a full experience no longer requiring repair or correction. My imagination knows greater trust of my world as expectations melt away, giving rise to a new form - acceptance.

Stage 7. Celebration and Integration.

I now consciously celebrate the beauty of my own creations. In this stage there is a celebration for the variety of unique gifts that I offer myself, integrating the mirror of life into my beingness. This is the stage of full empowerment – in which I take full responsibility and power over my life and environment. This is the stage of I AM – I AM all that I perceive. This is the stage of knowledge – knowing that it is I who create my life and I who is the cause of my life. This is the stage of oneness - all "selves" are integrated into one great whole. Higher Self is no longer hidden by fear as fear is replaced with trust and power. This is the authority of the creator in full possession of awareness of that creative power.

Beyond stage 7 is the great unknown territory of spirit. This is not the religious "spirit" of fear and control so many have used to enslave and dominate others. This is the spirit of total freedom and unlimited power. It is the spirit of ecstasy, bliss, and total love.

The journey of the soul through these stages is a wondrous journey of self discovery. Perhaps you recognize yourself in one of these stages. Take the opportunity of recognition to move on and progress to the next stage. With recognition, you are 99% of the way to completion. Your own happiness and the happiness of those around you depend upon you. You are the central character in your drama. It is up to you to choose. It is up to you to take charge of your life.

It is up to you…

Some Common Thinking Errors and What to Do About Them

It's Normal to Be Different

We are all extraordinary, all strange, all freaks, every last one of us. Some of us just happen to be more notable, with a particularly interesting story to tell.

In nature, biological systems operate within the context of their environment. According to evolutionary theory, systems either adapt to their environment or die off. Freaks of nature sometimes become the dominant species because they can adapt better than those we consider "normal" or not freaks.

As humans we are intensely interested in freaks of nature. They are interesting – and we are curious. All too often, we want to "fit in" and "just be normal" – yet doing so would likely make us dull and uninteresting – not special – boring.

Although we like to "fit in" and "be normal" we also like being "special" to someone or to a group. Some people confuse being special with being a freak – although freaks are certainly special, you don't have to be a freak to be special.

Each person on the planet is unique – no one else on earth has your unique combination of nature and nurture – how your specific genetic pattern has adapted to your specific environment.

You don't have to work at being special – it is who you are already.

The issue is not whether or not you are special. The issue is that we sometimes fail to recognize that specialness and celebrate it in a meaningful way. And sometimes we fail to recognize the ways others acknowledge our specialness.

To begin with, when you recognize your own uniqueness, your own specialness, you tend to interpret environmental signals based on that specialness. You tend to support your acknowledgment with more acknowledgment – no need to "try" to become special by doing extraordinary things – like acting in a freakish way.

You already know you are special – no need to prove what is already proven.

When you extend that feeling of being special to others you care about, you tend to reinforce their feelings of specialness. It is the very definition of conditional love – extending love feelings based on who someone is or how they act.

Humans are conditional. Get used to the idea!

A young college student, Susan thought she was defective because she just "didn't fit in". She struggled with self-image but always felt that she somehow stuck out like some kind of circus freak. "So, then, if you don't like people staring at you, why is it that you wear your hair spiked and wear so much body piercing jewelry?" I asked. "Because it makes me feel unique...." And so she was.

The problem, Susan discovered as we progressed, was not so much that she didn't fit in as it was that she didn't appreciate her innate uniqueness. She also realized that the way she was expressing her uniqueness was imposing a price she was less and less willing to pay – the price of lone-liness and exclusion. Although she loosely fit into a sort of society of similarly marked individuals, she felt isolated and alone – and unable to connect with someone in a meaningful way for her.

After dealing with the negative aspects of her loneliness, she began to entertain new notions about herself and where she really wanted to go with her life within the framework of the greater societal picture. Once she "got it" that she was unique no matter what she wore or did, she could then focus more on how that uniqueness might fit into and benefit the society she wanted to embrace.

Weeks later, I bumped into Susan at a local Costco. I didn't recognize her. Gone were the gaudy nose and eyebrow piercing jewelry. Gone were the multicolored spikes in her hair. Gone, too was the bold makeup and exotic clothing. Instead, I met a woman who had a unique sense of hu-mor and delightful personality.

Her new "way" of being who she is makes her stand out enough to be appreciated while her willingness to accept others around her, including what we might call societal norms, helps her connect more deeply with those she cares about most. She is still as unique as she ever was. Yet now she's accepted her uniqueness in a way that suits her emotional needs a little better than before.

Horse and Rider

When I was much younger (and oh, so much more foolish…), I rode a horse once or twice. I noticed that as I rode the horse, I could pull the reins one way or another, kick the horse, or pull back on the reins and the horse would respond with movement in the direction I chose – and applied the correct action – and, most importantly, if the horse agreed.

This worked quite well until about half way through the ride when the horse got wind of the barn and the oats. Then I experienced trot, gallop, and full out run – no matter what I did with the reins or spurs. So far as the horse was concerned my only purpose in life was to make sure he got exercise when he wanted it, oats to eat when he wanted it, and a safe, warm place to eat and sleep when he wanted to do that.

My brain is like that. At the base is an animal brain, called the reptilian brain – the horse. Atop it sits the limbic system – the saddle. And atop that sits the neocortex – the human rider(s) – two of them, like husband and wife, left and right hemispheres. Sometimes they agree with each other while other times they disagree – which matters not one iota to the horse as long as it gets its oats on time.

The purpose of the horse is to survive – to either feel good (pleasure) or escape pain. It bases all its thinking on evaluation of threat or benefit. Its language is sensation. It is an animal, after all.

The purpose of the riders is to direct the horse toward a goal determined by the riders. However, for almost all humans (nearly 100%) – almost all the time (nearly 100%) – **the goal of the riders is to satisfy the horse!**

Check it out for yourself – why do you do most of what you do in life? It is to either feel good (pleasantly satisfied) or to escape pain (or some painful, unpleasant outcome). You look at your environment, your world, in terms of what may threaten you (either physically, psychologically, or "spiritually") or what may be of benefit (to you or those you care about). **That's the horse's job**!

Basically, from that point of view, we are animals with big brains – capable of rising above the animal mentality yet choosing, instead, to use our huge mental capability – our capacity for more – to satisfy our "inner animal." We are riders enslaved to the horse. We are so used to this arrangement that we defend it and fight any other way.

Compassion?

Consider your relationships with other people. There really is no "them" – there is only your interpretation of your own animal signals that you ascribe to "them." You use your magnificent neocortex to imagine how you would feel in their condition and impose that image upon them. We like to call it compassion, but I wonder if it is merely our animal predictions – using our big brains to satisfy the horse again based on our interpretation of cause-effect. We want to see a victim and we want to be the hero that saves the day. I want to be Frodo – the guy who beats the odds and vanquishes the evil lords and their dark hordes.

When we "fix" someone else's problems, we are merely satisfying our need to fulfill our own animal needs (to be safe, secure, free from pain, and satisfied) – needs we interpret as lacking in others (externalizing in order to satisfy our own need to feel safe, secure, free from pain, and satisfied ourselves).

Proxy, surrogate, or distance healing can be the purest form of compassion when applied in a non-judgmental way. It's just that, for the most part, I am unwilling to be non-judgmental because that would mean acting in freedom from the horse – independent from my need to satisfy the animal within. I'd have to be completely willing to forgo my own survival – willing to risk death – for anyone else, rather than only those I judge worthy of my sacrifice – which judgment would tend to perpetuate the horse enslavement in myself and others.

I'm not sure I can even conceive of what it is like to no longer serve the horse. I don't know if I have ever been there – I'm so used to being in its service. Therefore, at this point in my life, I accept that I am in the service of the horse – a condition borne of the evidence before me.

By my acceptance of this condition, I also accept that my interpretations of my experiences of life are askew – favoring the horse rather than objective reality. I accept that I may not recognize "enlightenment" or "freedom" if or when it may occur because of my dogged attention to the horse. And, let me be clear about this – I am not seeking enlightenment or freedom! Because I don't even know what they are, I can't seek them.

Some Common Thinking Errors and What to Do About Them

If I choose to seek, I can only seek using my current criteria – which is based on serving the horse. Do you get my drift? Catch-22…

It seems to me that the only way to gain freedom from the horse is to kill the horse – psychologically. I believe it is possible. It's just that I may have to overcome my dislike for pain and my need for comfort.

However, due to the fact that I am human and have the capacity for higher intelligence thought along with an inquisitive disposition, I can question my interpretations and motives.

And, even while serving the horse, I can at least enjoy the ride.

Some Common Thinking Errors and What to Do About Them

Transformation?

Are you good enough for transformation? How do you know?

Why do you want to transform your life? Just what is it you think is going to be better than what you are experiencing now? Why do you think transformation is what you want? Why do you think that transformation is the answer? And what is the question that you feel transformation will answer? And where did you get your question – did you come up with it yourself or did you inherit it from someone else – an authority perhaps?

What do you intend to transform into? Will you be richer? Taller? Shorter? Have a slimmer body? A better job? Will you look like a super model? Maybe you will have that "perfect" relationship? What is your standard you feel you don't meet? Is it your standard or did you inherit it from someone else – an authority perhaps?

How will you know that you have transformed when you do? What measuring device will you use? Will you simply satisfy some animal need to feel pleasant or escape pain? Will you achieve some diploma or certificate that tells the world that you have "made it"? Will you wear the robes of authority or possess the trappings of success? What is your measuring device – is it yours or did you inherit your measuring device from someone else – an authority perhaps?

Do you have some purpose in life that you must attain in order to feel that you have succeeded? What is that purpose? How do you know if you are on the path of that purpose? What are your indicators? Can you fake that purpose until you make it? If you look like you have achieved your life purpose does that mean you have achieved it? And once you have achieved your life purpose does that mean you can stop pursuing it? Where did you come up with the idea that you have a life purpose? Did you establish this by yourself or did you inherit it from someone else – an authority perhaps?

What if the journey is the destination? Could it be? And if it were so that the journey of life is the ultimate destination of life, then could you say with surety that transformation is necessary? Do you think you can know the destination of life – where it should go? And where did you get your should, your knowledge? Did you make up your shoulds yourself or did you inherit them from someone else – an authority perhaps?

Some Common Thinking Errors and What to Do About Them

Are you good enough for transformation? How do you know?

I wonder… and I question… until I'm sure… I don't know… anything at all…

The beginning of knowing is also the end.

"The mind is so powerful that it can create an experience to support any belief. Then we believe the experience proves the belief, not knowing that the belief created the experience." Krishnamurti

Some Common Thinking Errors and What to Do About Them

What Are You Afraid Of?

Some years ago, my wife and I were invited to do a fire walk. We built a BIG fire – over 8 feet tall and 20 feet across we stacked the wood – then burned it down to a 15 foot round bed of hot coals. It was so hot in fact that we burned our faces from several feet back.

Sure it's possible to walk on coals – lots of people have done it before and not gotten so much as an ouch of a burn. But I had not done it before – and even after the first person walked across – and even though we knew scientifically and spiritually that it was possible – the HEAT and FIRE coupled with our own past experiences with fire – I had been burned badly on my feet in a fire in the garage in our old house – confronted us with the real possibility of serious injury.

FIRE BURNS FLESH!!! My body knows it – which is why I don't put my hand on the hot stove on purpose. My body knows about heat and knows how to react to it – mostly by AVOIDING IT.

I don't care how much you believe you can do it – when you stand at the precipice and your face and arms are burning from the heat – you are face to face with one of the greatest inbred fears of animal-kind – the fear of fire – ala Frankenstein's monster. All animals are afraid of fire – including humans. Fire is TERRIFYING.

What would it take to make me step from the cool grass onto the super-heated hot coals?

In my case, it was curiosity. I was SO driven by curiosity that I walked right across – the second person across after the host. I'd have been first if we did not honor the host with being first.

Curiosity → Motivation → Firewalk

I've seen and heard "experts" who complain that a firewalk is no big deal because physics will take care of you. Others have written that it's some kind of mystical spiritual power that protects the walker. I don't care what "power" or physical law makes walking on fire possible. That's not the point of the walk. The point is to overcome your fear. And I will tell you from personal experience, that first step is FULL of doubt

Some Common Thinking Errors and What to Do About Them

and apprehension – FEAR. There is a REASON firefighters wear protective clothing – you don't find them going barefooted into a burning building.

What did I learn from walking on fire?

- Not everything I fear is insurmountable.

- When I'm face-to-face with deathly fear, I may be on the precipice – just a few steps across the coals away from success.

- As I was burned slightly on the first crossing, after the third crossing, I realized that I would be okay even though I was burned the first time.

- Until my foot touched the coals, it was just theory.

- The hotter the coals, the better the walk across them.

- I (and my body) am more powerful than I once believed.

Courage is when you feel the fear and do it anyway. Courage? It didn't seem like it to me at the time. We just DID WHAT HAD TO BE DONE. But it WAS courageous because we felt the fear and did it anyway.

I satisfied my curiosity.

The very next year, I rappelled out of a helicopter for the first time. My fear of heights kicked in BIG TIME when I peeked over the edge to see the ground SO far below me. Still, I made it down the rope to the ground with no trouble at all. And just to really face my fear of heights, I did the rappel Australian style – facing toward the ground – fast. It was terrifying – and exhilarating. I repeated the performance three more times that day for good measure. The third time was so much fun!

At age 13, my son rappelled for the first time – down a 60 foot wall. It was terrifying for him – the scratch marks at the top of the rappel tower bear witness to his terror. Humans fear falling – and will avoid it ferociously. Once he got through the terror, he was like a kid with a new toy – you could not keep him off the wall. Suddenly, his fear had become his friend. And he was fundamentally different after that experience.

Some Common Thinking Errors and What to Do About Them

Space Mountain

Our daughter, Amanda, was six at the time we visited Disneyland in Anaheim, California. When she saw Space Mountain she became very excited and had to go in and ride the ride. She was barely tall enough to pass the height/age requirement for the ride so the staff insisted she ride with an adult. When it was her turn, she got into the ride car with her daddy (me). She was so excited she could hardly sit still.

Space Mountain is a dark roller-coaster and as we sat in the dark we heard the clickety-clack and felt the jerking movement of the car but saw nothing as we began to rise on the first leg of the coaster.

We reached the top and all was well with Amanda. Suddenly, without warning, we were over the top and careening through the caverns of Space Mountain at breakneck speeds in the dark. Just as suddenly, Amanda became a wildcat: scratching, gouging, and screaming to get off the ride. Too late! The car was in motion and there was no getting off. No matter how much Amanda wanted off that ride, it was in motion and could not be stopped.

Doing all that I could to keep Amanda in the car and warding off her sharp fingernails, it was the longest 30 seconds of our lives! After what felt like an eternity, the car slowed to a stop, the lights came up, the car doors opened and, trembling, I stepped out of the car.

Turning to help Amanda out, I saw she was still in the car. With eyes the size of dinner plates, she looked up at me and exclaimed, "Wow, dad! That was great! Let's go again!"

In that moment, I learned some valuable lessons about life:

1. We're having the time of our lives and maybe we'll awaken to that realization and really enjoy the ride of life!

2. No matter how much we scratch, gouge, scream, or plead to get off the ride of life, it's in motion and there is no getting off until it comes to a complete stop.

3. As we find later that we really were having a great time, why not become aware of and celebrate that now?!

4. Sometimes when life seems the scariest, we're having the most fun!

Some Common Thinking Errors and What to Do About Them

5. A 30-second ride can feel like an eternity until we realize how much fun we're having - then, whoosh! It's over in a flash.

6. Awareness is the key to joyous living.

And then there is the story of how we faced the terror of excommunication from our religion – which meant facing our fear of eternal oblivion – and became different people as a result. Lost friends? Some, maybe. Worth it? Absolutely YES!!

Some Common Thinking Errors and What to Do About Them

Gifts from Our Ancestors

In the course of evolution, people with certain genes fared better than others – and because they survived, they passed on their genes, making the general population more like them. For example, Europeans who came into contact with and yet survived the great plague did so because they had a genetic advantage over their neighbors. Because more of them survived to pass on their genes, their descendants tend to show that same genetic factor.

Unfortunately, a genetic advantage in one era or age (like the Ice Age) may be a killer in another (like now). More body fat in an Ice Age man made him more likely to pass on his genes; whereas today it could prevent him from doing so.

What genetic factors are a problem in your life? Do you have a predisposition for certain diseases or conditions (physically and psychologically)? How can you know which conditions or diseases are genetically affecting you? How can you make a change that has a higher probability of success on a genetic level – if it is possible at all?

There is a fundamental interaction between genetics and how our brains process the genetic information. We create and maintain brain circuitry based on a genetic blueprint modified by experience/learning (environmental factors). It's a delicate balance between nature and nurture. Neither genetics nor conditioning completely rule our life experience – rather, we experience the result of an interweaving between the two – kind of like the weaving of DNA.

To make a genetic change, we must make a FUNDAMENTAL choice to BE a different way than we have been in the past AND we must back it with environmental support. "How do we do that?" you might ask.

The first important factor here is in the sense of BEING. You must first choose to BE a different way and then back it up with committed ACTION (Doing). Then you'll HAVE a new genetic factor.

Do you want to be healthier? Then BE healthier in your mind and ACT upon that inner sense. For example, who would you BE if you were 20 pounds thinner? How would you feel? What would you BE then? Imagine that "sense" of BEING and then DO – act as if you ARE that way already. If you then look in the mirror and say to yourself, "Geez! I've been thinking thin but I'm just as fat as I was before..." – you've not yet taken on the BEING of thinness – you've only toyed with it; maybe tried it on, but have yet to BE thin in your mind.

Acting healthy means simply going with the sense of being thin. You don't have to work at this – you will enjoy it because it is natural to you. For example, a thin you might enjoy a brisk walk or modeling clothing in the mirror – so do it and KNOW in yourself that you ARE thin. After a while, your mind will start a chain reaction in all the cells in your body and they, too, will BE thin.

It's a good idea to get your physician behind you when it comes to body changes, though, as there is a lot you may not know about your own body that your physician might know better.

It's in your genes – so take control TODAY. Naturally...

Some Common Thinking Errors and What to Do About Them

On Success and Failure

What if you could be guaranteed of success at ANYTHING you did? What would you do differently?

Before you answer, let's take a moment to consider the relationship between success and failure.

You are always successful at everything you actually DO. AND – you are always successful in NOT doing what you don't do.

What you do may not match your desire. And, your environment may give you the impression that you have failed at something. Yet, because you have actually DONE SOMETHING, you have succeeded in doing that something, whatever it is. Likewise, for those things you do not do, you have succeeded in not doing them.

Because your actions always bring about successful outcomes, intent and desire become all the more important – because you tend to focus your creative action in the direction of your true intent – and get outcomes associated with it – rather than on your desire no matter how strong your desire may be.

Problems can arise because we often don't know our true intent. We **think** we do, though, and that poses a specific problem – one we call failure. Desire is based on what we think is our true intention – and because we believe we know our mind, we marshal inordinate emotional energy to desire rather than surrendering to true intent.

Failures are outcomes based on what we **think** are our true intentions. HOW you perceive the results of your actions can lead you to better understand and use your true intentions.

If you are seated, you are not standing. One could say that you succeeded in sitting while you failed to stand. However, in the very next moment, you could reverse that and find that you succeeded in standing and therefore have failed at sitting (because you are no longer seated while you are standing).

Actually, though, you have succeeded at sitting AND standing – just at different times. AND, you have succeeded in NOT sitting while standing and NOT standing while sitting.

Some Common Thinking Errors and What to Do About Them

Maybe it's more about what you choose to view as success that makes the difference – because you are always – ALWAYS – succeeding at something – in every instance.

It seems to me that it is impossible to fail. EVERYTHING you have done in your life you have successfully done – otherwise you would have succeeded in not doing it – or succeeded in doing something else.

IT'S ALL IN HOW YOU PERCEIVE YOUR SUCCESS.

Is the cup half empty or half full? Answer – neither and both! The cup is completely full with SOMETHING – air and liquid… and completely empty of everything ELSE.

"Do not try and bend the spoon. That's impossible. Instead, only try and realize the truth."

"What truth?"

"There is no spoon."

"There is no spoon?"

"Then you will see that it is not the spoon that bends. It is only your-self."

- The Matrix

Eye and Body Movement for Problem Solving

A study appearing in the journal Psychonomic Bulletin & Review[4] is the first to show that a person's ability to solve a problem can be influenced by how he or she moves.

"Our manipulation [of the body] is changing the way people think," said University of Illinois psychology professor Alejandro Lleras, who along with Vanderbilt University postdoctoral researcher Laura Thomas, conducted the study. "In other words, by directing the way people move their bodies, we are – unbeknownst to them - directing the way they think about the problem."

"The results are interesting both because body motion can affect higher order thought, the complex thinking needed to solve complicated problems, and because this effect occurs even when someone else is directing the movements of the person trying to solve the problem," Lleras said.

According to Lleras, this type of consciousness, "embodied cognition," describes the link between body and mind in a new and insightful way.

"People tend to think that their mind lives in their brain, dealing in conceptual abstractions, very much disconnected from the body," he said. "This emerging research is fascinating because it is demonstrating how your body is a part of your mind in a powerful way. The way you think is affected by your body and, in fact, we can use our bodies to help us think."

In one experiment dealing with a problem in knot tying, subjects were more successful if they swung their arms than if they stretched their arms. "By making you swing your arms in a particular way, we're activating a part of your brain that deals with swinging motions," Lleras said. "That sort of activity in your brain then unconsciously leads you to think about that type of motion when you're trying to solve the [knot tying] problem."

According to Llares, previous studies have demonstrated that body movement can assist in learning and memory or can change a person's perceptions or attitudes toward information.

Other studies by Lleras and his colleagues have shown that directing a person's eye movements or attention in specific patterns can also aid in solving complex problems. This is the first study to show that directed movements of the body can, outside of conscious awareness, guide higher-order cognitive processing, he said.

"We view this as a really important new window into understanding the complexity of human thought," Lleras said. "I guess another take-home message is this: If you are stuck trying to solve a problem, take a break. Go do something else. This will ensure that the next time you think about that problem you will literally approach it with a different mind. And that may help!"

Some Common Thinking Errors and What to Do About Them

The Impact of Imagery on Perception

Research from Vanderbilt University has found that mental imagery—what we see with the "mind's eye"—directly impacts our visual perception. The research was published online June 26 by the journal Current Biology in a paper titled, "The Functional Impact of Mental Imagery on Conscious Perception."

"We found that imagery leads to a short-term memory trace that can bias future perception," says Joel Pearson, research associate in the Vanderbilt Department of Psychology. and lead author of the study. "This is the first research to definitively show that imagining something changes vision both while you are imagining it and later on."

"These findings are important because they suggest a potential mechanism by which top-down *expectations or recollections of previous experiences might shape perception itself*," Pearson and his co-authors write.

"You might think you need to imagine something 10 times or 100 times before it has an impact," says Frank Tong, associate professor of psychology and co-author of the study. "Our results show that even a single instance of imagery can tilt how you see the world one way or another, dramatically, if the conditions are right."

The authors' new findings offer an objective tool to assess the often-slippery concept of imagination.

"It has been very hard to pin down in the laboratory what exactly someone is experiencing when it comes to imagery, because it is so subjective," Tong says. "We found that the imagery effect, while found in all of our subjects, could differ a lot in strength across subjects. So this might give us a metric to measure the strength of mental imagery in individuals and how that imagery may influence perception."

The findings may also help settle a longstanding debate in the research community over whether mental imagery is visual—that one imagines something just as one sees it—or more abstract.

"More recently, with advances in human brain imaging, we now know that when you imagine something parts of the visual brain do light up and you see activity there," Pearson says. "So there's more and more evidence suggesting that *there is a huge overlap between mental imagery and seeing the same thing.* Our work shows that not only are imagery and vision related, but imagery directly influences what we see."

Some Common Thinking Errors and What to Do About Them

Thinking and Feeling Make Perception

First, perceiving something does not make fact.

A study[5], published in the September 2009 issue of the journal *Psychological Science*, "addresses the age-old question: 'Do we see reality as it is, or is what we see influenced by our preconceptions?'" Study coauthor Piotr Winkielman, professor of psychology at the University of California, San Diego adds, "Our findings indicate that what we think has a noticeable effect on our perceptions."

We're talking about the relationship between what we believe and what we experience. Our thinking goes: "I perceive an event and the way I perceive it is THE way it happened. Further, the way I feel about the event has nothing to do with how the event went down."

Thinking error!!

"We imagine our emotional expressions as unambiguous ways of communicating how we're feeling," said coauthor Jamin Halberstadt, of the University of Otago in New Zealand, "but in real social interactions, facial expressions are blends of multiple emotions – they are open to interpretation. This means that two people can have different recollections about the same emotional episode, yet both be correct about what they 'saw.' So when my wife remembers my smirk as cynicism, she is right: her explanation of the expression at the time biased her perception of it. But it is also true that, had she explained my expression as empathy, I wouldn't be sleeping on the couch."

You mean, if I change my mind about my interpretation of the data, the event changes for me? Whoa! That's radical!

"It's a paradox," Halberstadt added. "The more we seek meaning in others' emotions, the less accurate we are in remembering them."

Oh, and, by the way – the less accurate we are at interpreting them, too!

"The novel finding here," said Winkielman, of UC San Diego, "is that our body is the interface: The place where thoughts and perceptions meet. It supports a growing area of research on 'embodied cognition' and 'embodied emotion.' Our corporeal self is intimately intertwined with how – and what – we think and feel."

Well, I guess we really do see (and hear, smell, taste, feel) what we believe! And at the root of it all is our body. We give lots of kudos to our magnificent minds, but when you really get down to brass tacks, our body plays a much bigger role than we give it credit – it has the starring role!

This adds significant credibility to my own theory about emotional healing – it's in the body! Sensation is the language of the body. We ignore our body's language at our peril – getting fatter, more stressed, and less resilient. I wonder what would happen if we were to focus emotional healing processes on the physical aspects of those emotions – the physical sensations that arise during the expression of our emotions. We might find the key to healing our emotions and our mental constructs that hold those emotions in place. Maybe my theory is worthy of study, too.

Some Common Thinking Errors and What to Do About Them

The Power of Your Affirmations

A member of the United States Senate, known for his hot temper and acid tongue, exploded one day in mid-session and began to shout, "Half of this Senate is made up of cowards and corrupt politicians!"

All the other Senators demanded that the angry member withdraw his statement, or be removed from the remainder of the session.

After a long pause, the angry member acquiesced. "OK," he said, "I withdraw what I said. Half of this Senate is NOT made up of cowards and corrupt politicians!"

Did you notice how both of the Senator's iterations meant the same thing? How many times have you confused yourself with negative affirmations? For example, how many times have you told yourself that you could not do something. Most of the time, such self-defeating affirmations are absolutely false. You aren't telling yourself the truth.

For example, maybe you've told yourself that you can't stop smoking. The truth is, of course, that you really CAN stop smoking, you just don't want to. Maybe you've told yourself that you can't possibly get that big contract because… [dozens of reasons why not]. The truth is, you're AFRAID you won't get the contract. Or, you believe it is UNLIKELY you'll get the contract.

The truth is – we don't know all the possibilities. We too often settle for the tiny bit of information we have at hand believing we have ALL the necessary information to make a solid statement of truth. "I can't live without her…" Bullsh*t! Of course you can live without her – you just don't like your vision of how life would be then.

Reason dictates that we consider possibilities – rather than settling on one. It's the quantum measurement problem in the macro world – whenever you settle on one possibility, the others tend to disappear, leaving only the one you choose. But it does not make it truth!

"Believe nothing. Entertain possibilities." – Caroline Casey

It's okay to settle on one possibility to the exclusion of others – it's the way of life. I'm not suggesting that you go against nature. Rather, I'm suggesting that you continue entertaining other possibilities after you have chosen one. Let yourself be open to alternatives. Rigidity of thought

Some Common Thinking Errors and What to Do About Them

– "I'm right!" thinking – tends to embitter one's life and sour relationships. Instead, when you are sure you are right, act resolutely yet be flexible enough to entertain alternatives.

You may just find that truth is not half what it's cracked up to be.

Some Common Thinking Errors and What to Do About Them

Feeling Low? Maybe It's OK

Feeling a bit low or blue during the winter months? Or maybe just feeling a little depressed now and then? Well don't despair or feel anxious over it – adding to the feeling. It's perfectly normal for humans to have mood swings – and to have negative moods that can last for days or even weeks.

The slightest shift in the balance between serotonin and melatonin, adrenalin and noradrenalin, and other chemicals in the body can affect moods – and it is NORMAL for us to do so and feel that way when we do.

According to University of East London psychologist Professor Mark Rapley, *"Bottling up anger and sadness is never a good way of dealing with things; problems tend to come back and bite us harder further down the line. The trouble is, we've become so obsessed with being happy that we now see being down as a real problem – when, in fact, it's perfectly normal.*

"We're constantly encouraged to be anxious about whether we are happy or depressed, yet these feelings are not illnesses, simply part of regular human experience. Life would be so much duller if we just muddled along in the middle without feeling any emotions at all. Learning to recognize that it's normal to feel angry or sad is a good thing for our mental health."

Balance is boring!

Feeling blue or "down" offers you a chance to reconsider – to ponder and reflect – and maybe take action to alleviate the blues. And in the course of solving the blues problem, maybe you'll come out with new ideas to make the rest of your life even better than before.

When I feel down, I sometimes think that "all is lost" or that "it will never end" or I just can't see me ever coming out of it. Such thoughts come from "absolute" thinking – which is normal when one is feeling under stress.

In reality, if I were to investigate, I'd notice that 99.99999+% of my life is going along wonderfully – and only the tiniest portion has gained my attention and is really "bugging me" – why? Because it is out of the ordinary!

Some Common Thinking Errors and What to Do About Them

Maybe the sub-par feeling is simply the result of something I ate – that changed my body's chemical state to the blues. If I will reconsider my mood tomorrow morning when my body chemistry has had time to change, maybe things will look differently, too – and probably will.

However you are feeling right now, chances are you'll feel differently within a very few hours. Not necessarily because of environmental influences – rather, maybe due to just a slight elevation of a single chemical in the body.

Next time you feel blue, don't despair or worry – adding to your problem – it's probably simply a natural and normal mood. If it lasts for some time – several weeks perhaps – maybe then would be a good time to seek assistance from a qualified healer. First, though – make sure you're not just experiencing life as a human should – with moods, attitudes, feelings, and chemistry!

Some Common Thinking Errors and What to Do About Them

Rainy Days

During rainy seasons, there is the feeling that the rain will never end – rainy days are short and rainy nights are long – a sense of dreariness and depression overcomes many.

And yet there is a sense of hope – an expectation that the sun will eventually show itself again.

We experience seasons in our lives like that – sometimes it seems like years on end of rain. What keeps us going during those times is expectation – expectation that the sun will once again light our lives and warm our hearts - the kind of hope born of expectation based on prior experiences of success and accomplishment.

During the "rainy days" of our lives, I think it well to remember such days of success and accomplishment – because they tend to give us hope – hope that the "sun" will come out again. It's just a matter of time then until the sun once again appears and shows us the cornucopia of colors that beautifies our world and causes our hearts to sing.

RAINBOW

A rainbow in its golden form,

Is but the child of sun and storm.

When these two opposite have wed,

You see their offspring over head.

The thunder speaks in voice loud,

The sun except behind a cloud.

The wedding chamber is shut tight,

He woos his love thru all the night.

When morning comes she's loathe to rise,

He dances proudly through the skies.

And loudly shouts to all the earth,

That they will soon behold a birth.

Some Common Thinking Errors and What to Do About Them

Out of the mist he weaves black lace,

To cover his beloved's face.

Tall trees their heads in homage bow,

And the sun whispers "It is now".

And from her face the veil is torn,

And low! A rainbow has been born.

- Peggie Lorensen

On the "flip side" –

Some Common Thinking Errors and What to Do About Them

Something wonderful is about to happen!

I wonder what might happen if you chose today to CONSIDER that something wonderful is about to happen TO YOU! Just considering some positive motivational outcome tends to set up the energy for it to occur. You'll probably also want to let go of controlling just WHAT that wonderful thing might be – control is based on fear and tends to deflate positive motivation.

Each day, awake with the expectation that, "something truly wonderful is about to happen to me, and maybe today is the day…". When the mail arrives, get excited about it – each piece of mail might be "it". When you answer the phone, be aware that "this might be it!"

We tend to get what we think about and focus attention upon. Want some excitement and joy in your life? Focus attention on it by anticipating it – get giddy about it.

Then set it up to happen again by expressing gratitude to the universe for supplying what you wanted when something wonderful does happen (and it will, I'm sure!). Get really clear about letting go of how it has to look or how it has to happen to get you to accept it – be open to surprise.

Something wonderful is just about to happen TO YOU! Maybe today is that day…

(*Thanks to Wendi Friesen, CCHT at wendi.com for this idea.*)

Some Common Thinking Errors and What to Do About Them

Chapter 2

Conscious Thinking Errors

Along with Some Ideas about Them

"An error does not become a mistake
until you refuse to correct it."
- John F. Kennedy after the failed Bay of Pigs invasion.

Some Common Thinking Errors and What to Do About Them

10 Common Thinking Errors

And What to Do About Them

Based on the work of Aaron Beck and others[6], David Burns outlines 10 common mistakes in thinking, which he calls cognitive distortions.

1. **ALL-OR-NOTHING THINKING** – Also called Black and White Thinking - Thinking of things in absolute terms, like "always", "every" or "never". For example, if your performance falls short of perfect, you see yourself as a total failure. Few aspects of human behavior are so absolute. Nothing is 100%. No one is all bad, or all good, we all have grades. To beat this cognitive distortion:

   Ask yourself, "Has there ever been a time when it was NOT that way?" (all or nothing thinking does not allow exceptions so if even one exception can be found, it's no longer "all" or "nothing")

   Ask yourself, "Never?" or "Always?" (depending upon what you are thinking)

   Investigate the Best-Case vs. Worst-Case Scenario NLP Meta program[7]

2. **OVERGENERALIZATION** - Taking isolated cases and using them to make wide generalizations. For example, you see a single negative event as a never-ending pattern of defeat: "She yelled at me. She's always yelling at me. She must not like me." To beat this cognitive distortion:

   a)   Catch yourself overgeneralizing

   Say to yourself, "Just because one event happened, does not necessarily mean I am (or you are or he/she is...[some way of being])"

   Investigate the Big Chunk vs. Little Chunk NLP Meta program in which one tends to focus more on either the "big picture" or on the details.

3. **MENTAL FILTER** - Focusing exclusively on certain, usually negative or upsetting, aspects of something while ignoring the rest. For example, you selectively hear the one tiny negative thing surrounded by all the HUGE POSITIVE STUFF. Often this includes being associated in negative ("I am so stupid!"), and dissociated in positive

Some Common Thinking Errors and What to Do About Them

("You have to be pretty smart to do my job"). To beat this cognitive distortion:

  a) Learn to look for the silver lining in every cloud

Count up your negatives vs. your positives – for every negative event, stack up a positive against it. Make a list of both negative and positive character attributes and behaviors.

Investigate the Associated/Dissociated NLP Meta program – seek to be associated in positive and dissociated in negative. To associate means to be "in" the experience – first person (I or me). To dissociate means to experience from a distance – third person (they or them).

4. **DISQUALIFYING THE POSITIVE** - Continually "shooting down" positive experiences for arbitrary, ad hoc reasons. In this way you can maintain a negative belief that is contradicted by your every-day experiences. The good stuff doesn't count because the rest of your life is a miserable pile of doo-doo. "That doesn't count because my life sucks!" To beat this cognitive distortion:

  a) Ask yourself, "So what does count then?" "In what way?"

Accept compliments with a simple, "Thank you."

Make lists of personal strengths and accomplishments

5. **JUMPING TO CONCLUSIONS** - Assuming something negative where there is actually no evidence to support it. Two specific sub-types are also identified:

  a) Mind reading - assuming the intentions of others. You arbitrarily conclude that someone is reacting negatively to you, and you don't bother to check it out. To beat this one, you need to let go of your need for approval - you can't please everyone all the time. Ask yourself, "How do you know that...?" Check out "supporting" facts with an open mind.
  b) Fortune telling - anticipating that things will turn out badly, you feel convinced that your prediction is an already established fact. To beat this, ask, "How do you know it will turn out in that way?" Again, check out the facts.

To beat this cognitive distortion:

Some Common Thinking Errors and What to Do About Them

a) When the conclusion is based on a prior cause (for example, the last time your spouse behaved in this manner s/he said it was because s/he felt angry so s/he must be angry this time, too), ask yourself, "What evidence do you have to support your notion that s/he feels..." "How did you arrive at that understanding" "What other conclusion might this evidence support?"

b) When the conclusion is based on a future consequence ("I'll die for sure if she keeps harping on this...") Ask yourself, "How does this conclusion serve you?" and "If you continue to think that way... [what will happen to you]?" and "Imagine 5 years from now..." (Future Pace)

6. **MAGNIFICATION & MINIMIZATION** - Exaggerating negatives and understating positives. Often the positive characteristics of other people are exaggerated and negatives understated. There is one sub-type of magnification or Catastrophizing - focusing on the worst possible outcome, however unlikely, or thinking that a situation is unbearable or impossible when it is really just uncomfortable: "I can't stand this." To beat this cognitive distortion:

a) Ask yourself, "What would happen if you did [stand this]?"
b) Ask yourself, "How specifically is [this/that/he/she] so good/too much/too many/etc. or so bad/not good enough/too little/etc.?"
c) After asking question b., ask yourself, "Compared to what/whom?"

7. **EMOTIONAL REASONING** - Making decisions and arguments based on how you feel rather than objective reality. People who allow themselves to get caught up in emotional reasoning can become completely blinded to the difference between feelings and facts. To beat this cognitive distortion:

a) NLP Pattern Interrupts and new anchors are the most powerful state changers - interrupt anything negative: "X makes me mad" "How does what I do cause you to choose to feel mad?" Interrupt: "How could you believe that?"

8. **SHOULDING** - (Necessity) Must-Can't thinking. Shoulding is focusing on what you can't control. For example, you try to enlighten another's unconscious - they *should* get it. Concentrating on what you

Some Common Thinking Errors and What to Do About Them

think "should" or ought to be rather than the actual situation you are faced with will simply stress you out. What you choose to do, and then do, will (to some degree, at least) change the world. What you "should" do will just make you miserable. To beat this cognitive distortion:

a) Ask, "What would it feel like, look like, sound like if you could/did or could not/did not?" or, "What would happen if you did/didn't?" or, "What prevents you from just doing it then?" or, "What rule or law says you/I SHOULD?" or, "Why should I?" or, "Could you just prefer instead?" or, "Why SHOULD I/YOU?"

b) Investigate the Match vs. Mismatch NLP Meta program in which a person's attention is draw by that which is the same (match) or that which is different (mismatch).

9. **LABELLING and MISLABELING** - Related to overgeneralization, explaining by naming. Rather than describing the specific behavior, you assign a label to someone or yourself that puts them in absolute and unalterable negative terms. This is a logic level error in that we make a logic leap from behavior/action ("he called me a name...") to identity ("therefore, he's a jerk"). To beat this cognitive distortion:

a) Ask yourself, "What could be a better way of looking at this that would truly empower you/me?" or, "Is there another possible more positive meaning for this?"

b) When you recognize you are labeling or are being labeled, ask, "How specifically?" Example: "How specifically am I a jerk?" – which will evoke behaviors rather than identity.

c) Remember who you/others are in spite of behaviors: "Even though I failed the test, I'm still a worthy person."

d) Investigate NLP Logic Levels. Logic Levels are basic structures of personality arranged according to a hierarchy. The basic levels are identified as:
   • Spiritual
   • Identity
   • Belief
   • Capability
   • Behavior

10. **PERSONALIZATION & BLAME** - Burns calls this distortion "the mother of guilt." Personalization occurs when you hold yourself personally responsible for an event that isn't entirely under your control. For example, "My son is doing poorly in school. I must be a bad mother..." and "What's that say about you as a person?" - instead of trying to pinpoint the cause of the problem so that she could be helpful to her child. When another woman's husband beat her, she told herself, "If only I were better in bed, he wouldn't beat me."

Personalization leads to guilt, shame, and feelings of inadequacy. On the flip side of personalization is blame. Some people blame other people or their circumstances for their problems, and they overlook ways that they might be contributing to the problem: "The reason my marriage is so lousy is because my spouse is totally unreasonable." – instead of investigating their own behavior and beliefs that can be changed. To beat this cognitive distortion:

a) Ask, "How do you know [I am to blame]?" "SAYS WHO?"

b) Ask, "Who/what else is involved in this problem?"

c) Ask yourself, "Realistically, how much of this problem is actually my responsibility?"

d) Ask, "If there was no blame involved here, what would be left for me/us to look at?"

e) Investigate the NLP Self/Others Reference Meta program in which a person's attention references either oneself or another.

- Self Reference is the selection of evidence and criteria based on reference to one's own perceptions, beliefs, values, etc. For example, a person using Self Referencing would know when they've done a good job at work, and might say something like, "I know I did a good job." And when challenged about their work they might say, "That's your opinion." [my reference opinion is correct]

- Other Reference is the selection of evidence and criteria based on reference to the perceptions, beliefs, values, etc., of others. For example, a person using Other Referencing would know they've done a good job when they heard someone else say, "You've done a good job," If challenged about the job they might answer, "I wonder what I did wrong." [someone else's reference opinion is correct]

These 10 cognitive errors are all habits of thinking that are deeply ingrained. The good news is, like any habit, these patterns of thinking can be broken and discarded through awareness and practice.

The experiences you have
reflect what you believe about them.

Some Common Thinking Errors and What to Do About Them

Overweight?

In the USA obesity – body mass index above 30 – is pandemic. My sense is that the "problem" has become societal as well as personal. Morgan Spurlock's "Supersize Me" illustrated one important fact – fast food can make you fast fat. Our wealthy society has created a situation where most Americans under-exercise and overeat. Further, our lifestyles of cubicles and computers and fast food mean many Americans don't see the kitchen for weeks on end.

On the psychological side, there is the ever-present push here for you to eat more. Every other TV commercial is about food – the others are about cars – and all use thin, sexy models to sell their wares.

> *American Marketing Scam #1 – If you LOOK sexy, you must BE qualified, good enough, smart enough, honest enough, or whatever enough... – deserving of whatever it is you want.*

And that leads me into the "model" thing. Every study I've ever seen on "beauty" shows that women (and men, too, to a much lesser degree) get better treatment when they are thinner. If you look sexy, you must BE qualified, good enough, smart enough, honest enough, or whatever enough... – deserving of whatever it is you want. Which accounts for why we are so easily conned – we tend to trust our visual/sexual channel rather than our intellect/logic channel.

On TV, which programs score high and remain popular? The ones with the "babes" of course. And we as a society have this belief that celebrities are automatically role models and authorities – which is why many companies hire them to pitch their wares and so many become politicians.

We don't get it that media celebrities, especially thin, curvaceous female ones, are intended to sell products – everything from movies to fashion-ware to dish soap. They are not suddenly wiser or smarter than we because they become a TV or movie celebrity – they are merely marketing objects. They may have great talent and drive but that is not what got them to celebrity status – marketing did. And marketing is big business.

I see two ends marketing to support the other today – one side markets pleasure – those things that pile on the pounds and hurt our health. The other side markets the cure for those things. This is what is called a crossfire zone in the military – and in a crossfire zone, everyone DIES. I believe that if you buy into the marketing ploys you see on TV, you will die. The "buy to make yourself feel better" pie is poisoned!

The only reasonable choice I see for overweight women is to learn to genuinely love and appreciate themselves for the valuable people they are – and to get it that looking sexy (read "thin and young looking") does not make you smarter or more enlightened or more qualified (unless you just happen to be a porn star, of course), or more valuable.

It might make you more desirable to the opposite sex – maybe – for a while perhaps – which is fine if that is all you want from life – a short period of acceptance for your body alone. But what about engaging and lasting relationships? What about heart connection relationships? What about real relationships that nurture the soul through a lifetime – relationships where trust, value, and mutual respect reign… for generations…

I believe that if you want to find and address the real issues behind your overweight condition, watch and listen to your favorite overweight stand-up comedian when they talk about their weight – personally I like Kirstie Alley and Chris Farley (deceased). Their material is funny alright, and so true!

Part of your being thinks it's funny, but a significant part of you does not – that part says, "Ouch! That hurts to hear!" Inner conflict gets the cortisol flowing and that packs on pounds. Stop the conflict and a significant element of the overweight issue dissolves away – with the fat it tied up in your body. When all of your being can laugh at the jokes, the conflict will be over and the good chemicals will flow naturally and easily.

Some Common Thinking Errors and What to Do About Them

The Addictive Mind

And what to do about it!

"I've had this addiction for 30 years. I know it's killing me but I can't quit. I want to, but I just can't. I know myself - I'm too weak."

As a practicing Hypnotherapist, I've heard it a gazillion times. The excuse that one has had the addiction for X number of years somehow justifies their inability to stop or quit the habit.

As many as 80% of cigarette smokers who stopped smoking did so on their own without any interdiction whatsoever. That means no patches, no gums, no hypnosis, nothing but their own will power - cold turkey. Even smokers who had smoked for decades.

The Great American Smoke Out was intended to be "the day" for smokers to stop cold turkey. And cold turkey is by far the best way to kick any substance abuse addiction. An alcoholic, for example, would stop being an alcoholic if s/he were to stop cold turkey and never take it up again.

Why, then, does it seem so hard to stop?

It has to do with your animal brain - that part of you that only understands one thing - survival. The belief is that pleasure equates to life and survival - while pain equates to death or non-survival. It seeks pleasure and avoids pain. That's its job. And it will do whatever it feels is necessary to accomplish its ends - keeping itself alive and well. It has no ethics and is completely immoral - having no moral sense at all. It doesn't care who gets hurt so long as it gets its next hit - which it believes it needs to survive.

It's an animal.

What has happened in the case of an addiction is that the animal brain has associated your substance abuse with pleasure - survival. That's why it protects the addiction so strongly. The animal part of you craves survival - the substance. Since it believes that it MUST have the substance to survive, it will produce "convincer" language for you - those little lies in your head that take you back into your habit. You know them - "Oh, just ONE won't kill you..." and "You're just too weak to quit..." and "It's going to hurt too much to stop..." etc.

Some Common Thinking Errors and What to Do About Them

It will also create body sensations to convince you that you must go along with it and not stop. The fear of withdrawal is the strongest urge to continue in smokers. That fear presents itself as physical body sensations - lots of them. From body weight gain to jitters to bitchiness, your animal brain will do what it needs to do to continue the addiction and preserve your life - at least that's what it believes.

Your animal brain will do or say whatever it takes to convince you to continue.

The animal brain has your body sensations and autonomic functions at its command. What it does not have is command of your will, volition, or interpretive centers. YOU are in charge of those. The animal can present you with pain - but it's a lie. It has really just presented you with SENSATION. You interpret the sensation as pain, or withdrawal, or whatever negative you assign to the sensation. It is just a sensation - that's all.

You can change your interpretation.

To make cold turkey work for you - just learn to accept sensation as sensation. If you assign the label "pain" to every sensation you don't like, after a short while, you will find yourself uncomfortable, in pain, and seeking relief from the "pain." That will most likely push you inexorably back into your addiction - or possibly a new one.

Even before you attempt a cold turkey stop of your addiction behavior, you can practice reassigning your sensations from "pain" to "sensation." Simply tell yourself with conviction that you are about to stop using [your addiction substance] forever and notice the sensations you experience. Exaggerate the sensations if you can so as to further acknowledge them.

Remember - it's just sensation - that's all.

You can do the same with other sensations. Instead of a "headache" for example, describe the headache to yourself without using the word, "pain." Do the same for all other sensations associated with the headache - maybe neck muscle strain, etc., and stomach discomfort - which you may further describe as pressure, gurgling, nausea, or whatever - as objective as you can get.

Objective descriptions are comprised of reports from your senses - sight, sound, feeling (sensation), taste, and smell. Avoid judgments or

Some Common Thinking Errors and What to Do About Them

justifications ("becauses") - simply describe the sensation in terms of your 5 senses. For example, "painful stinging sensation in my wrist" is easier to say but much less objective than, "a bluish brown area about 1 inch in diameter 1 inch above the right wrist, palm side, perhaps a half inch below the surface of the skin, that I feel as a sharp localized sensation when I move my wrist up and down."

Avoid trying to diagnose your sensations - associating them with some cause. Just describe them. That's all. Avoid, for example, saying "my wrist hurts because I hit my wrist on the table..." Focus on WHAT rather then WHY.

Once you make the commitment and stop your addiction behavior - do the same exercise to mediate and relieve withdrawal symptoms. Withdrawal symptoms are just the animal's way of getting you to return to your safety zone - back into your addiction - where it believes you need to be to survive.

Again -

Your animal brain will do or say whatever it takes to convince you to continue (your addiction).

Remember - your animal brain is mistaken about what you need - yet it is convinced that it is right - and it is doing its job the best it can to help you survive. The only problem is that it is wrong. By acknowledging it by using its own language - the language of sensation - describing your sensations rather than interpreting them - you lovingly help your animal brain return to sanity - and let go of the addiction that is killing you.

You can use this process with only slight variation to assist you in changing your weight, too - in connection with a good weight management program.

Tip - IF you believe that your addiction is a disease you will never overcome - you are right. And you will struggle all your life and never overcome it.

If you believe that your addiction is a symptom of misguided associations and errors in thinking - that can be corrected instantly - you are right! And you will live your life in freedom.

Which belief would you prefer to model?

Some Common Thinking Errors and What to Do About Them

Note: I acknowledge with great admiration the work of Jack Trimpey, LCSW, author of *Rational Recovery: The New Cure for Substance Addiction.* His web site is www.rational.org where you can find additional resources.

Unknown Outcomes?

During the years I worked with a local physician, I learned from him that physicians struggle with the same "insecurity" I did - that is, he often prescribed a course of treatment that did not appear to work. I spoke with him occasionally during those years about this apparent discrepancy between treatment expectation and actual outcome.

His basic philosophy, which he learned while at med school and during his internship and which I agree with, was that you can't possibly account for every possible patient treatment outcome. Physicians deal in probabilities. It is probable that a specific treatment will work for a patient based on past experience with that treatment for those particular patient symptoms - but it is just plain unreasonable to think it will work for every patient exhibiting the same symptoms every time - or predict exactly how an outcome of treatment will appear in a specific patient.

If, for example, you were to win the lottery today, you can't predict precisely what your life would look like next week or next month or next year. You might be living on the Riviera in a luxurious home overlooking the beach - or you might be busy fighting to keep your newly acquired fortune away from greedy relatives, scam artists, or thieves - or you could lose it all in a stock market crash. At best, you can only guess at a probable outcome!

The same goes for treatment - the best predictor for treatment is past performance [of that treatment for that set of symptoms on patients similar to the one being treated]. However - due to the uncertainty principle, you can't know right now with total surety what your life will look like even in the next second.

That could leave us with quite a sense of insecurity about our future. Remember, though, that the future is not totally unpredictable - only *uncertain*. That means the *probabilities* are predictable. Based on our actions/behaviors we can predict with fairly high certainty - but not absolute certainty - a *probable outcome.*

In the course of therapy or treatment, we hope that by the time we achieve our intended outcome, we are a different person than we were when we set the goal. Our frame of reference changes - making it much more difficult to notice changes when they occur. We might not recognize change when we see it.

Some Common Thinking Errors and What to Do About Them

So - when a change therapy seems to make no difference in your life, take a moment to consider what a change *could* or *probably* would look like rather than what you think it *should* look like. You may be pleasantly surprised.

Some Common Thinking Errors and What to Do About Them

Changing Behavior in Others

Imagine that someone behaves towards you in a way that you don't like. You have a variety of approaches regarding how you respond.

One set of approaches deals with your own area of responsibility. You might ask yourself, "What is it about me that has allowed, permitted, drawn certain people to behave towards me in this way?"

The answers to this question may reveal one of two kinds of answers. The first is the opening of opportunity. Looking like a victim often attracts predators of some description.

Another answer or approach is more metaphysical. For example, say that someone is being very stubborn and not accepting your point. Some metaphysical schools of thought would have you examine yourself, to see if you do this kind of thing to others. Are you sometimes stubborn about some things? Do you sometimes refuse to see the points of some others?

A third approach is to look at the other person. Is this a typical pattern of behavior for them? Do they do this kind of thing often, with your and/or with other people? If this is the case, then you can take steps to remedy the situation.

These approaches are not separate, and can operate simultaneously. And if you turn these approaches into a checklist of three simple questions, you can turn just about any unwanted behavior from another into an opportunity for achieving more of what you want.

There is a new woman at work who I sometimes find quite bothersome. When being instructed in a new task, she often rushes ahead to the next step without waiting, and usually gets it wrong. She could so easily get things right if she just waited for the next instruction.

So I can run through my checklist of questions:

1. What have I been doing to allow this behavior? What can I do differently to promote the behavior that I want her to have?

2. Do I ever do this to others? Do I rush through things without waiting for the next instruction? Do I ever jump the gun prematurely, and if so, where and when, and how do I change myself to be more careful, more thorough, and more attentive?

Some Common Thinking Errors and What to Do About Them

3. Does this person do this with other people and situations? If it's not isolated to me, then it's a more general behavioral pattern. Can I change it so that it's different, at least with me? If I can't change it, how can I avoid it or minimize my contact with it? And if I can't change it or avoid it, how do I accept it and move on?

It's a simple set of questions, and I think that it can be very useful vehicle for catching what you don't want and turning it into something you do. So where do you use this? Well, how many places in your life have people behaved towards you in a way that you haven't liked? What kind of insights and new tactics can you get from asking these questions with all those situations? And how many ways does this new way of analyzing the situation give rise to getting more of what you want?

As for me, the answers to these questions have already proven very useful and enlightening, both for my own development and other things.

(Elroy Carter, Mindlist. Used with permission.)

Some Common Thinking Errors and What to Do About Them

Time for a Change?

Research out of MIT's McGovern Institute for Brain Research, shows that brain neurons can change in as little as two minutes even in adults. For years scientists have known about the plasticity of the brain – that it can change neuronal connections and even grow new brain cells. But until recently, no one had studied the speed at which these changes can occur.

It is unlikely that a brain cell would grow to maturity and make all those dendrite connections in just two minutes. Some other mechanism must be at work.

"…we think the connections were already there but were silent, and that the brain is constantly recalibrating the connections through short-term plasticity mechanisms," explains senior author Nancy Kanwisher.

That makes sense – the brain simply holds cells and connections in reserve – a sort of brain cache in which brain cells lay dormant but ready to snap into place when called upon. Kanwisher: "Our study shows the stunning ability of the brain to adapt to moment-to-moment changes in experience even in adulthood."

What does that mean for you? It means you CAN make those life changes you want to make. And you can make them literally in the blink of an eye. Given the right stimulus, your brain circuitry can make near-instant changes – which, in turn, can change your behavior, your perceptions, your will, and your results.

Maybe you feel you are now ready to make a change but are afraid it will take a long time or will require lots of expensive therapy to achieve. That may be true – and maybe not true. The only way to find out is to give it a try – experience a change therapy and see if maybe you change literally in the blink of an eye.

The worst that could happen is that you don't get the results you want from that particular therapy or therapist. If that is the case, try another therapy or a different therapist. Don't give up! When a therapy model and therapist "clicks" with you, change can be virtually instantaneous. That's really good news!

You can do it – your brain can help!

Some Common Thinking Errors and What to Do About Them

Problems with "Ah ha!"

Have you ever suddenly "got it" and said to yourself, "Ah ha!"? Maybe you felt you suddenly came to some realization that would solve your current or life problems.

Many new therapists believe that if a client comes to a "realization" or "ah ha" then all is well and the client will come away from the session with resolution. This presupposes the misconception that if we just know enough about our problem we can solve it and that resolution means solution.

"Ah ha's" are fine and often make you feel you are progressing toward your goals. And sometimes that feeling is right on and correct. However, just as often or more, the "ah ha!" is merely the mind's way of keeping you stuck or in the status quo – no progress toward substantial change.

When I was doing Rapid Eye Technology trainings I'd often see students light up with "ah ha! I get it now!" and then return to doing exactly what they were doing before. Their mind formed an image or "lock-on" – and with the lock-on they would lock out whatever else seemed different from their image. It's called a scotoma and it feels very good – releasing endorphins in the brain. It is NOT resolution, though it often feels like it.

A scotoma is merely the result of the mind fixating on ONE solution or ideal – which feels like resolution – and excluding all other possibilities. In other words, being RIGHT.

Rightness (the condition of being right) is not all it's cracked up to be. Being right when you're wrong is just being VERY wrong – along with all the attending defenses to sustain the wrong as right – that wonderful feeling of "I'm superior" and somehow better than. It is the height of foolishness to believe we know anything. We merely hold notions as beliefs and then apply rightness to those notions we like – seeking or sustaining pleasure while seeking to escape pain (as we suppose). Therefore, rightness actually comes down to "that which makes me feel good or safe about…[some thing or concept]" while wrongness is "that which I feel might threaten or cause me pain."

"Ah ha!" can sometimes lead us down the path of rightness – along with its associated narrowing of choices. Once we "get it" in a great "ah ha!" we tend to close down to alternatives and be satisfied with our "resolution" – which is really a justification that makes sense to us because it fits into our image of what <u>should</u> be. Since we are satisfied, we tend to plateau rather than seek real resolution and what is beyond. And at the end of the day, we are left with neither resolution nor satisfaction.

I'm reminded of the two elderly women out driving one beautiful morning – both could barely see over the dashboard. Cruising along they came to an intersection. The stoplight was red but they just went on through. The woman in the passenger seat thought to herself, "I must be losing it, I could have sworn we just went through a red light."

After a few more minutes they came to another intersection. Again the light was red and again they blew right though it. This time the woman in the passenger seat was almost sure that the light had been red but was really concerned that she was losing it. Getting nervous she decided to pay very close attention to the road and the next intersection to see what was going on.

At the next intersection, sure enough, the light was definitely red. As they went right through it, she turned to the other woman and said, "Mildred! Did you know we just ran through three red lights in a row! You could have killed us!"

Mildred turned to her companion and whispered timidly, "Oh my gosh! I'm driving?!!" (A senior "Ah-ha" moment)

Some Common Thinking Errors and What to Do About Them

When "Why" Is the Wrong Question

Sometimes the word can serve us – as in times when we are seeking a philosophical answer to a philosophical question, like, "Why is space so vast?" etc.

However, usually we confuse "why" with useful words like "what" and "how".

"What" tends to elicit a noun – some <u>thing</u>.

"How" tends to elicit a behavior or action – something we <u>do</u>.

"Why" tends to elicit a justification or reason – our philosophy.

"What is for dinner?" elicits nouns like "carrots and peas" and "fish" and is quite a different question from "Why isn't dinner on the table yet?" – which tends to elicit a justification.

"<u>How</u> can we work out our differences?" elicits an action with some kind of end result in mind – and is far different from, "<u>Why</u> can't we work out our differences?" – which focuses attention on the reasons why we can't. It may be nice to know why you can't work out your differences – but don't you really just want to <u>do</u> something about it rather than just know why?

Particularly when applied to ourselves, "why" can be the incorrect question. "Why do I always push away those I love most?" Although this question may elicit some interesting information – what I call "Gee Whiz" information – which in this case would probably include some kind of "ah ha" like "So THAT'S why I do that!" – does it really get me any closer to a real resolution or, better, a solution?

More likely, what I will elicit with my "ah ha" will be some kind of justification for "why" I have done what I have done – which tends to keep me safely in my current behavior pattern. If what I really want is a solution, then perhaps I would do well with a "how" question instead – eliciting a <u>strategy</u> for successful change.

A more useful question might be, "How can I behave to attract and keep others interested in me?" Or, "In what ways can I change my behavior so others feel safe around me?"

Some Common Thinking Errors and What to Do About Them

"Why" can be useful if it puts you onto a path toward the kind of substantial and real change you seek. When your "why" question leads you to an "ah ha" moment, don't let it fool you into believing you've come to a resolution or transformation.

Transformation can only be measured in behavioral change over time. "Ah ha!" is simply gee whiz information if it doesn't lead to substantial behavioral change over time.

Don't let your "Why's" beat your "What's" and "How's" into submission.

Here's one way you can take charge of your "why's".

Since "why" is a mind game, we'll play a mind game to control it. Somehow that sounds reasonable to me…

Whenever you hear yourself speak the word "why" in your mind make a "what" or "how" question of it instead. For example, "Why did you do that?" becomes "What did you do?" or "How did you do that" or "What can I do to help you stop/keep doing that?" or "How can we stop/encourage more of this behavior?" etc. Get creative – by getting creative you open the parts of your mind that might conceal the answers you seek but have been beaten into submission by your misuse of "why" questions.

Some Common Thinking Errors and What to Do About Them

Why?

"He who has a why can endure any how." Friedrich Nietzsche

I appreciate how important it is for us to have an answer or some kind of reason for why things happen as they do. We invent religions and gods and theories of all kinds to help us cope with what we don't understand or fear. Even science has its own religion of sorts - always seeking to find that illusive reason why.

I, too, would love to know why. It's in my nature. Although questioning is important, asking the right question is much more important - and difficult to do. In lieu of proper questions, I've often settled with poorly formed questions along with answers I've settled upon and defended - answers to the wrong questions or a question asked wrongly. Further, I have tended to put "reasons" behind my settled upon answers - a means by which I can protect my "truths" and make them seem right no matter their veracity. We call this process justification or rationalization.

For a moment, let's dispense with all reasoning, justification, and rationalization and simply look at cause and effect. Something happens and that causes something else to happen.

> *Although questioning is important, asking the right question is much more important – and more difficult to do.*

Some cause and effect relationships we have experienced often enough that we feel that we can predict effect from cause.

For example, if I step off the step, I fall to the ground. I'm familiar with the action of gravity on this earth and I can expect to fall to the ground every time I step off the step. Further, I can predict with fair accuracy that if you step off the step, you, too, will fall as I did.

Physicist David Boehm showed that cause and effect is all an illusion, though, because all causes are entwined with all effects in a mesh so tightly woven that it is literally impossible to separate cause from effect - we just believe that we can - it makes us feel safer to know that we can know cause from effect.

This is "if-then" thinking and we all do it - it is our nature. We like to accurately predict - it makes us feel right – and safer. Even when we accurately predict hurt, it somehow feels better because we were right about our prediction.

Some Common Thinking Errors and What to Do About Them

That leads me to cheating. We are great humans but lousy scientists overall. That is, as humans, we like to be right rather than correct. I will tend to "fix" the outcomes of my experience to make me look more right - rather than accepting what is as correct. To that end, I tend to set myself and others up so that I will more likely make myself look right. I'll cheat if I have to!

And then there are…

Reality Tunnels – The "Only" Fallacy

Cause and effect thinking tends to tunnel our thought processes over time. That is, we believe one thing happens because of another – then we tunnel that cause-effect relationship into an "only" relationship. One thing happens only because of another.

Reality Tunnels have the form or structure of:

X causes Y

Therefore – (Reality Tunneling)

Y must be caused (only) by X

What if Y is caused by Z? Or X+Z or X-Z? Or something else entirely? According to many quantum physicists, causes and effects are so entwined together it's impossible to separate one from the other. Basically, there is never one cause for one effect or one effect for one cause. Perhaps reality is a big mess when it comes to cause and effect. To imagine that there is only one cause for any given effect tends to deny reality.

Certainly it seems cause and effect works differently than we think it does. We think we know the cause and/or the effect, when, in fact, the best we can do is deduce one from the other.

When we use reality tunnels, we save some thought energy but tend to neglect or overlook viable and equally compelling alternatives.

I've noticed that it's common practice to use reality tunnels to keep beliefs in place. For example, in the movie Joan of Arc, Joan saw everything that happened as a sign from God to join the revolution. She used her reality tunnels to hold her faith in place. Every effect she observed simply led her to one and only one conclusion.

In other words, it is possible to "bend" reality to suit our beliefs. All we have to do is assign a cause to an effect – we do it every day. When our presupposition, our "come from", is a certain way or thing, we will tend to tunnel our "becauses" to justify and support it, just as Joan did. We use "only" to help us – "It could only be caused (because) by God…" for example. This is just another way we work to keep ourselves safe in our rightness, rightness that Joan of Arc called "righteousness."

I've heard people complain, "You're making me angry." This presupposes that I'm the <u>only</u> reason and there is no <u>other</u> reason they're feeling angry. Acting upon this reality tunnel can cause quite a bit of relationship damage.

What if, for example, another reason they are feeling angry is because their hormones are out of balance due to ingestion of some food that disagreed with them?

What if, for example, yet another reason they are feeling angry is because they had a hard day at work?

What if...

What if...

What if...

Settling on just one and only one reason tunnels out all the other and possibly reasonable alternatives. What if the entire situation were due to something entirely different than you had supposed. What if your deduction is incorrect? What then?

You're never angry for the reason you think. – A Course in Miracles

"Never attribute to malice that which can be adequately explained by stupidity." - Hanlon's Razor

"You have your way. I have my way. As for the right way, the correct way, and the only way, it does not exist." - Friedrich Nietzsche

How do you get out of reality tunnels? Well, you don't. But you can learn how to use them to your advantage...

Some Common Thinking Errors and What to Do About Them

The Golden Setup

Let's consider a cause-effect reality tunnel example: the common cold. You know what happens. Somebody coughs, you breathe in, within hours or days you start feeling symptoms – scratchy throat, difficulty breathing, achy muscles, fever, etc. You've caught a cold.

Structure:

Blame model -

- You've caught a cold
- Because...
- You saw a friend cough last night and it's "going around..."

Responsibility Model -

- You've caught a cold
- Because...
- You coughed and it's "going around..."

-THEREFORE-

You must...

- Act sick
- Get confirmation from your physician
- Treat the disease with pharmaceuticals or alternatives
- Take time off
- Etc.

Never mind that cold symptoms take days to develop. Never mind that the cough could be the result of any number of things other than a cold. Never mind that maybe it's not even a cough at all. Once you've made up your mind to tunnel your reality in this manner, you've set up the cause and the effect. The only thing left is for nature to take its course – and it likely will.

Unless...

Some Common Thinking Errors and What to Do About Them

Suppose for a moment I want to experiment with what happens when I change a small part of the cause-effect relationships I have assigned to a cold? What if now I want to introduce a new element into the equation? I want to introduce a setup - a new "reason" for the cold - a new purpose. I want to exploit my cause-effect reality tunnel in the case of a cold.

Just allowing the introduction of a new element into the equation sets me up for possible change in how I experience a cold. I am primed for a new or different outcome. In NLP language, I'm messing with my presuppositions to achieve a new outcome - a "frame-up."

In my experiment, I tell myself that my cold is no longer a sub-par condition - that is, I am no longer "under the weather." Rather, I tell myself that the purpose of the cold symptoms is cleansing or body energy realignment, or mind-body belief system adjustment, or proxy clearing, or even weight adjustment processing.

I have elevated in my mind the <u>purpose</u> of the cold symptoms from *recovery from disease* to some *positive function* - part of my weight reduction regime, for example. I've assigned a new frame for the symptoms I collectively call a "cold."

Now, when I see the weight loss, my new cause-effect relationship is "When I experience these symptoms it is part of the overall weight reduction my body does as a result of my weight management plan and goal." This is just as valid a cause-effect relationship tunnel as my previous one that basically said, "My body is reacting to a disease element that is invading my body."

From a purely results oriented viewpoint - without any value or moral judgments - which cause-effect relationship reality tunnel would you consider more useful in a weight management regime?

Some Common Thinking Errors and What to Do About Them

Sandy Foundations

"If aliens did land in France 10,000 years ago... (the word "did" pre-supposes something), then the marks on the rocks have to be those of their space ships... (because that is the only option we'll entertain)" BASED ON THAT FACT, "Similar spaceship marks have been found on every continent and nearly every country... (a reasonable conclusion)" THEREFORE, (because the "if" expressed earlier is true) "we must consider what we must do to prepare for the inevitable time when they contact us..." etc.

"If... then" ==>evolves to become ==> "Because... then..." ==> "...and because of THAT... then..." ==>"...and because of THAT... then..." ==> ad infinitum... - creating long lines of belief truth connections where perhaps relationships don't actually exist - and neither does the truth.

We then base future beliefs on these and thousands or perhaps millions of other faulty "if... ...then" "because... then" non-relationships. We misrepresent, erroneously attribute, and incorrectly reference all the time - and then base future understandings and "truths" on those thinking errors. It's not that we are stupid - we just make human thinking errors. Just because we have big brains doesn't automatically mean we know how to use them, ya know!

In most cases these trains of beliefs are started when we were very young. It's not our fault that as very young children we believed everything we were told. We made an observation or had an experience we didn't understand - which is reasonable for a baby - and then in an effort to make sense of our world, we attributed what seemed like a reasonable and rational cause to what we experienced, or we were told some "truth" by an adult who themselves didn't know either. The problem is, our brains simply don't have the capability to make correct "cause-effect" relationships until we are much older. By then, we've already established our underlying "truths". Catch-22.

I was watching the TV last night. It was a favorite of mine - Ancient Aliens. I don't know if I want to entertain the possibility of aliens visiting earth - maybe it is true, maybe not - the evidence I've seen so far hasn't convinced me either way. The interesting part for me is not the theory or the "evidence" - it's the presentation of the theory as if it were true (much like religion). The basis should be considered - IF the theory

Some Common Thinking Errors and What to Do About Them

is true, THEN the evidence means this or that. BUT - and this is important - IF the theory is NOT true, THEN the evidence means something entirely different.

IF there is a God, then the observations I make concerning nature mean this or that. But IF there is NO God, then that same observed phenomena means something entirely different. It's not the evidence that is suspect - it is our interpretations I'm questioning. "IF" does not mean "BECAUSE". The question then becomes "IF there is a God... then..." rather than "BECAUSE there is a God... then..." Basing your life on "because" rather than "if" feels secure and certain when in reality, "because" is the sandiest of foundations.

Oh, and one more thing - people have been known to lie.

The Scotoma Solution

A scotoma is a mental situation in which one locks on to one idea and excludes all others – known as the "lock on and lock out" principle. We all do it – it's our human way of avoiding overwhelm when faced with too many choices. However, a scotoma can get you into trouble as we shall explore here.

In a Spongebob Squarepants cartoon, Spongebob gets up one morning and thinks he'll create a fantastic dessert for himself. Unfortunately, his choice of ingredients causes him to have horrific halitosis (bad breath). Spongebob proceeds to go outside, where he meets several people, all of whom scream and run away from him as soon as he opens his mouth and says, "Hello."

His conclusion – "I must be terribly ugly!" (faulty deduction)

Based on his erroneous conclusion, he weighs all evidence only in light of his conclusion – discounting evidence to the contrary. Every experience he encounters only tends to strengthen his belief that he is ugly rather than stinky. He has locked onto one idea and locked out all others – a scotoma. His scotoma causes him to feel less and less self-confident until he at last introverts and avoids others.

Spongebob's close friend, Patrick, who as a starfish, has no nose, can't smell the bad breath and so assumes his friend is correct in his assumption that he is ugly. Together, Spongebob and Patrick attempt to overcome the "ugliness" through a series of humorous, yet reasonable, methods – reasonable, that is, if Spongebob really were ugly.

They try positive affirmations, "I'm ugly and I'm proud!" etc. Again, all their efforts are aimed at correcting what they believe to be the fundamental problem – that Spongebob is ugly.

At long last Patrick tries some of Spongebob's "dessert" and finds that he, too, has become "ugly." Everyone runs away from him, too, whenever he opens his mouth. When Patrick then speaks to Spongebob and Spongebob gets a whiff of the odorous mouth, he finally gets it that he's not ugly – his breath stinks – and together Spongebob and Patrick celebrate the fact that "we stink!"

This is a fine example of what happens when we make an erroneous conclusion from the data we observe. Compounding the problem of erro-

neous conclusions is that we make many of our life-determining decisions based on data we evaluated and made conclusions on when we
were VERY YOUNG or in our infancy – a time in our lives when we
were physically and psychologically poorly equipped to make such conclusions.

Further, we did not have sufficient data to make such life-determining
conclusions. And so we find ourselves living our lives today based on
erroneous conclusions of ambiguous data (life experience) we made long
ago – so long ago we don't recall them – but we are living them out now
nevertheless.

What do we do about it? How do I become aware of that of which I am
unaware? I'm even so unaware that I'm unaware that I'm unaware.
Egad!

Here's what I recommend:

Develop a healthy skepticism about your own decisions and decision
making processes. Question yourself often,

- "Am I sure about this?"

- "Could I be wrong about
  this/that/them/you/me/us?" etc.

- "What other reason might
  there be…"

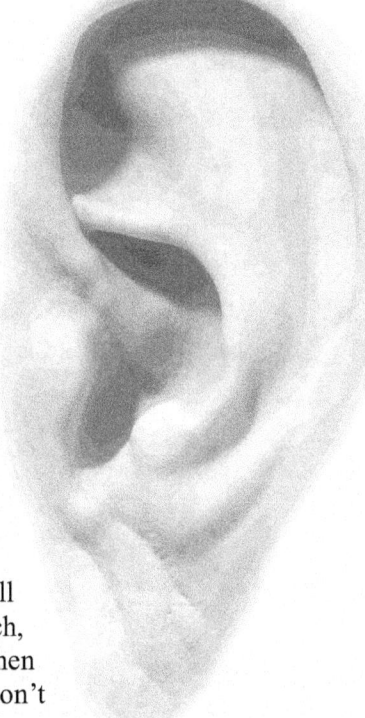

LISTEN to those closest to you. Consider criticism as golden nuggets of
awareness about that which you are
unaware. Spouses especially are gold-
goldmines for such info. Especially if
you feel threatened – the surest sign
that gold is afoot. Defending yourself
against your loved ones shuts the doors
and windows of awareness – genuine gratitude opens them.

LISTEN to your "enemies" – they will tell
you what you don't want to hear. As such,
they can be your best friends – at least when
it comes to information about you. You don't

Some Common Thinking Errors and What to Do About Them

have to give in or give up – just pay attention. "Could what they say about me be true – to some extent?"

Speak the words, "Thank you" to those you feel are attacking you. Be genuine – no sarcasm or brushing off. They are doing you a favor – it's just good manners to show appreciation. Besides, it shifts your thinking mode from emotion to reason – a good thing during communication.

Deal with your emotional triggers. I recommend you get help with them – to avoid missing those that hide from you. Seek out a therapist who works holistically – treating the entire being – someone skilled in rooting out those hidden emotional "secrets" that come forward when triggered.

Choosing – What Do You Want?

Oddly enough, for most people, this is the hardest part of manifestation – choosing what it is they really want – consciously. Sure, it seems easy, like choosing which pair of shoes to wear today. Yet, when you really get down to making the choice, there may be some reality tunnel obstacles involved:

- If I choose this, then I can't have that.

- If I choose one way, I don't know if I will get something else I want, too.

- If I choose to do one thing, I can't do another.

- I don't know what I want.

- I can't make up my mind.

- I've made too many mistakes before. This will probably be another.

- Somebody always gets hurt.

- I'm not good enough to have what I want.

- And the list could go on and on…

Choosing what you want from life is really much easier than it appears. All the "obstacles" I've listed above come from the part of us that is happy with the status quo – the way things are right now – no matter how unhappy that makes us. "Stay with a sure thing."

That's the kind of thinking that kills the soul – stuck thinking. It comes from the basic belief that we are the victims of our environment, our heritage, our bodies, our weaknesses, etc. And that is a choice – you can choose to be stuck wherever you are.

With a little awareness, however, you might discover that you have the power and are making choices in every moment. It's just that you've grown so accustomed to choosing that you are unaware that you are doing it – you take it for granted.

Breath is a good example of how we take choice for granted. You can choose to breath in a number of ways, yet you habituate to one or two styles – usually survival breathing – just enough to get you by. And yet the choice is still there to choose another style of breathing – it just takes a little awareness on your part.

Even now, as you read this, you're now more aware of your breathing. The awareness was as easy as that.

To get the choice ball rolling, let's focus on changing your mind – taking accountability for your choices. That means becoming aware that you have choice, aware that you are right this instant (and every other instant) making choices; and that you may use your power of choice consciously in every moment.

Stop taking your choices for granted! Start noticing that you are choosing!

Let's play a little game to get you going -

Right now, choose to say to yourself, "I am choosing to breathe as I am breathing right now." Follow that statement up with, "I am choosing to sit here and read this book as I am doing right now." Follow that one up with, "I am choosing right now to blink my eyes, beat my heart, move my body, and digest my food as I am doing right now." Then, "I am choosing to feel [happy, sad, alone, joyous, whatever] just as I am doing right now.

"I am choosing to be, do, have, feel, just as I am doing right now because it is what I most want to be, do, have, feel right now.

"I am choosing!

"When I am in my unconsciousness (unawareness), I tend to make unconscious choices resulting in unconscious consequences – consequences that I cannot associate myself in a cause and effect relationship. Something happens to me and I feel that I did not choose this for myself. It's just that I've been so accustomed to making choices that I found myself unconsciously doing so – and, voila, I have a consequence or result I was unaware was based on my choice.

Now is the time for me to take accountability for my choices and own my world. I can only do so by owning my life. I make the choices, and I get the consequences or results of those choices. If I am unaware of my choices, I can simply look at the results (my current experience) and take

Some Common Thinking Errors and What to Do About Them

accountability – I am experiencing exactly what I most want to experience right now as I have chosen this." (or something to that effect)

Once you have taken back your power of conscious choice, you will then find it much easier to consciously choose your outcomes, paths, and journeys – and find yourself experiencing them with far more enthusiasm, excitement, and joy than you could even imagine otherwise.

What do you want?

Some Common Thinking Errors and What to Do About Them

How Well Is That Working for You?

"How well is that working for you?" Dr. Phil McGraw's famous question is the essence of Neuro-linguistics and makes some very important assumptions:

- That what you are doing *is* working for you... (note that he asks, "*How well* is that working..." rather than just "*Is* that working...")

- That you have the *ability to judge* how well it is working for you... (else he wouldn't ask you)

- That you have the *power* to make a change... (else he would not bother asking)

- That you are *getting something* of value from what you are doing now... ("How *well*..." assumes a gain of some kind)

The answer to the question holds the key to making a change. It's called <u>awareness</u>. You can't change that which you don't recognize and acknowledge.

Perhaps you don't know why your life is not working as you'd like it to work. Maybe you think your problems are the result of someone else's actions or fault. Maybe you are confused or angry or sad or afraid...

Whatever is going on with you, evaluating your strategy by asking this simple question, "How well is this working for me?" just might get you out of the blame game and into the solution game.

Shifting from "Being" (I am so unhappy) to "Doing" (I feel unhappy) is the shift from stuck to solution. Evaluating your current strategy is a powerful first step toward getting what you really want. It's also a great way to evaluate your progress.

Look particularly at what you are getting as a payoff for your behavior. Do others fear you – and it feels like respect? Does your fear justify inaction and lack?

To elicit your psychological payoff, ask yourself, "What do I need that this behavior gets for me?" That is your payoff. And it might be one of the answers to the question, "How is this working for me?"

Some Common Thinking Errors and What to Do About Them

Try it. The next time you feel unhappy, angry, frustrated, sad, alone, afraid, or out of control, ask yourself, "How is this working for me?" followed by "What is my payoff for this behavior?"

Then listen to your inner voice – and shift from BEING unhappy to, "What can I DO to change this situation?"

It might just make the difference between living a life of frustration and enjoying one full of joy and enthusiasm.

Some Common Thinking Errors and What to Do About Them

Memories and Your Future

"Our findings provide compelling support for the idea that memory and future thought are highly interrelated and help explain why future thought may be impossible without memories. Suicidally depressed people don't remember particularly what happened last month and they can't really tell you much of anything about what they envision happening next week." (Szpunar, 2009)[8]

We tend to live out our future thoughts in the present – something like self-fulfilling prophecies. Much of that is due to our self-image or sense of identity. Traumatic events – particularly those that occur repeatedly – tend to taint our self-image. Memory loss as part of trauma or other issues can leave us with no future – a situation in which suicide seems plausibly logical.

So it seems to me we have a double-whammy – two major parts of us working against us. When we want to achieve something important to us, we are faced with interference from our tainted memories and future thoughts.

What can you do about it? How can you lift the onus off your back?

Well, I hope it's fairly obvious.

Have or make better memories!

"How can I change things that happened to me?" you might ask…

I'd answer that rather than recalling what actually happened to you, you are instead remembering your interpretation of what happened to you. Further, your memories are tainted by more recent events that are similar in nature to the original events. Memories are based on perception rather than reality and are highly malleable, subject to distortion, misinterpretation, and outright deception.

Perception is made up of many elements of mind and body. For traumatic events, your body gets involved in memory in a special way – it remembers how it felt and behaved during the traumatic event and uses that "memory" to build future thought, including motivation and belief in success – as well as automatic behavior.

Perception is malleable – changeable. You can literally mold memory by changing your interpretation of your perceptions. Take charge of your perception of past events and you can take charge of your future.

One step toward taking charge of your perception is to understand how your perception works. Just how do you interpret the world around you?

Well, you engage a strategy.

Where did this strategy come from? For the most part, it came from your childhood – when you were inexperienced, uneducated, and undeveloped. If I were a CEO of a large corporation, I would not like to hire someone with those qualifications to lead up a project. But that is who is leading up your life project – unless you replace them.

Since that project leader is you, you can't very well replace yourself. But you can educate yourself. You can bring that project leader up to speed.

To start with, as the trainer, I think it wise to understand your "student." You'll want to train him according to his learning method rather than to an adult understanding method.

Let's start by looking at process – your thinking process. Then model a perception strategy that takes advantage of that process. We don't want to introduce confusion into the strategy if we can avoid it. Yet, it seems you may have already done so because of the answers you derived from the question, "How well is that working for you?"

Some Common Thinking Errors and What to Do About Them

Order of Logic Levels

Each of us has within us an order of logical processing. We don't, for example, put away the food before we eat it. To awaken the powerful knowingness within us, we need to ask the right questions in the right order. When we cross logic levels, we confuse ourselves and come up with wrong questions, which in turn elicit the wrong information. Acting appropriately to wrong information is the same thing as acting inappropriately.

It's all about asking the right question. To that end, let's consider a thought process that follows this order of questioning:

1) **What** (the experience of "it" - whatever "it" is)

   a) Evaluation - determine if further investigation is merited and worthwhile or useful

      i) Yes - continue to "how"

      ii) No - experience more or another "what"

2) **How** (how do you do the "what" part - for example, during a magic show you ask, "How did they do that?")

3) **Why** (close on the heels of "how" in some cases - "Why does that work like it does?")

4) **When, where, and with whom** (the application of environmental or contextual elements)

I want to be convinced first that something I experience (even down to the level of just "I wonder") merits investigation into how and why before I go into how and why. "Trivial" pursuit is when I get "how" and/or "why" out of order with "what" - for example, "how does my computer monitor work?" - I really don't care at this time - I only care that it DOES work (which invokes a what question - "what does it do?" "It works!").

However, when my monitor STOPS working - THEN I might be inclined to ask:

   1) What happened? - the monitor stopped working.

2) How does the monitor work? (perhaps if I know enough about how it works, I might be able to get back to the experience of a working monitor - and maybe keep it that way)

3) Why did it stop working? - is it within my power to fix it, for example? (maybe if I plug this thing back here back in, it will then again work...)

4) Where can I find help? Who might know how to fix this thing... etc.

NLPers may recognize the question levels as logic levels:

1) What - the "being" level - same as the "is" or "am" level of identity

2) How and Why - the "do" or "mechanics" level of behavior/skills

3) Where, when, with whom - the "have" level of environment/context

When we confuse the timing of questions, we confuse logic levels - "Why am I such a dunderhead?" - is an out of order logic level question.

First ask, "*Am* I a dunderhead?" - which is a "what" question.

IF the question merits further investigation (the care level is sufficiently high to merit further action)...

Follow with "How do I behave like a dunderhead?" (or "In what ways do I behave like a dunderhead?") - this elicits your definition of "dunderhead" and supporting behavioral evidence (which is probably hot up for you since you are considering it in the first place).

Follow that with "Why do these behaviors indicate that I am a dunderhead?" - this elicits your strategies for "dunderhead" and can really open up the possibilities for change.

Finally, ask, "When, where, and with whom do I behave in that manner?" - eliciting the specific environmental details - the mountain is a lot easier to move one shovelful at a time...

I suspect that most presuppositions are created by crossing logic levels - particularly when we confuse the "why" and "how" logic levels with the "what" level.

Some Common Thinking Errors and What to Do About Them

Timing, timing, timing.

- "What" questions tend to elicit awareness.
- "Why" questions tend to elicit content or story (justification and judgment).
- "When, where and with whom" questions tend to elicit context.
- "How" questions tend to elicit process or structure.

Logic Levels Leaps

Let's look at two logic levels, Behavior and Identity. Behavior is the level of action (do) whereas identity is the level of being (be). Many people run with the following logic level leap:

"I did poorly on my math test." (Behavior level isolated to one environment)

"THEREFORE"

"I'm stupid." (Leap to the identity level where change is difficult)

Some people take anything that they have done well or continue to do well and attribute it to outside forces (attempting to abrogate their responsibility). They say, "I got lucky." Or maybe, "It must have been fate." Or, "It was a fluke." Or, "It was God's will." As a result, they do not increase their own belief in themselves. They perceive all of their successes at the behavioral level. When something goes bad or horribly wrong, they integrate the result at the identity level. Consequently, they increase their belief in their own "incompetence".

Then there are those people who take anything that they have done well or continue to do well and integrate it into themselves at the identity level, thereby increasing their own confidence in themselves and their abilities. Anything that gets them less than stellar results they chalk up as a learning experience and an indication to do something differently (leaving it in the behavioral level). They perceive the action at the behavioral level where it belongs and choose to assign the positive aspects to identity level:

"I did poorly on my math test." (Behavior level isolated to one environment)

"THEREFORE"

"I will study differently in the future." (Properly leaving the negative aspects assigned to the behavior level where change is easy)

***

"I did well on my math test." (Behavior level isolated to one environment)

"THEREFORE"

Some Common Thinking Errors and What to Do About Them

"I am a success." (Leap to identity level)

To turn the negative pattern around, one must put the logical levels in their proper places and use them beneficially:

- Positive reinforcing positive identity

- Negative reinforcing change in behavior

The very awareness of logic levels and how we make logic leaps can help you use them beneficially.

Chapter 3

Subconscious Thinking Errors

Along with Some Ideas about Them

Cognitive Biases

As a human being, I'm proud to say I have biases. Having biases is what separates me from the machines I live with. Although it is debatable, I tend to believe that biases serve a useful purpose – to some degree. Knowing I have biases helps me communicate, make choices, respond, and live with far less stress.

To believe you are unbiased is to say you are inhuman or a machine. Admitting your biases helps you take charge of them. And in taking charge of your biases you can take charge of your life. Further, in understanding your biases and how they work you become a more useful and stress-free member of your society.

As you read the list of cognitive biases along with their variants, I hope you, too, will find some value. Maybe you'll notice some biases you didn't know you had. You can't truly gauge any of the biases you might be operating under since it's not possible to accurately observe a system of which you're a part. Still, you may be able to note biases you see in others and by association assign them to yourself – and maybe notice how you might operate the same bias you see in another.

A cognitive bias is any of a wide range of observer effects identified in cognitive science and social psychology including very basic statistical, social attribution, and memory errors that are common to all human beings. Biases drastically skew the reliability of anecdotal and legal evidence. Social biases, usually called attributional biases, affect our everyday social interactions. And biases related to probability and decision making significantly affect the scientific method which is deliberately designed to minimize such bias from any one observer.

A List of Cognitive Biases

1. **Bandwagon effect** – the tendency to do (or believe) things because many other people do (or believe) the same. "Everybody's doing it!" (so I should, too)

2. **Bias blind spot** – the tendency not to compensate for one's own cognitive biases. "I'm not bigoted! I just love [Black, Latino,

Irish, HIV positive, gay, rich, poor…] people – as long as they stay over there / don't marry my daughter / don't vote… etc."

3. **Choice-supportive bias** – the tendency to justify one's past choices with positive attributes that may or may not have existed at the time the choice was made. "The car I bought has a good warrantee… so I DID make the right decision."

4. **Confirmation bias** – the tendency to search for or interpret information in a way that confirms one's preconceptions or opinions. This is the "I am almost always right" bias.

5. **Projection bias** – the tendency to unconsciously assume that others share the same or similar thoughts, beliefs, values, or positions. This bias sets us up to assume we know how others feel or think without us asking. See the Seven Stages of Projection to Celebration on page 15.

6. **Self-fulfilling prophecy** – the tendency to engage in behaviors that elicit results which will (consciously or not) confirm existing attitudes and beliefs.

7. **Attributional Error** - the tendency to misidentify probable causes for effects. "He did that to me because he hates me – not because he had a bad day at work." This error also extends to blame where we misidentify the offending person – especially if that person is ourselves.

8. **Hindsight bias**, sometimes called the "I-knew-it-all-along" or "I told you so" effect, is the inclination to see past events as being predictable. This could also be called the Nostradamus Effect because none of Nostradamus' "predictions" were ever known or understood until after they occurred.

9. **Impact bias** – Also known as the "Drama Queen effect" it is the tendency for people to overestimate the length or the intensity of the impact of future feeling states. "If he says 'no' I just know I'll die of shame!"

10. **Neglect of probability** – the tendency to completely disregard probability when making a decision under uncertainty. This is the "even though it has happened to most folks, it won't happen to me" bias.

Some Common Thinking Errors and What to Do About Them

11. **Status quo bias** – the tendency for people to like things to stay relatively the same.

12. **Authority bias** – the tendency to place value according to the opinion of someone who is seen as an authority on the topic. This is sometimes referred to as the "Religious Bias". This is the basis for the placebo and nocebo effects.

There are many more biases, but these are so common, I wanted to mention them in this book to introduce the concepts. I'm sure you can identify with most if not all of them. Knowing you have a bias is most of the way toward controlling it.

Scams, frauds, swindles, and prejudice all take advantage of our native biases. When you recognize this, the scam will fail – allowing the victim of the scam to turn the tables on the perpetrators or at the very least avoid the scam altogether. Knowledge trumps deceipt.

Some Common Thinking Errors and What to Do About Them

Intuition May Reveal Your Biases

Researchers at Wellcome Trust Centre for Neuroimaging at the University College London have managed to image the brain while it processes subconscious subliminal cues. This is important because it demonstrates for the first time how our brain processes subconscious information. We often think of such information as intuition or inspiration from some external source when instead, it seems we develop these "signals" from within.

Dr. Mathias Pessiglione, lead researcher concludes, "We conclude that, even without conscious processing of contextual cues, our brain can learn their reward value and use them to provide a bias on decision making."

Decision bias?

I think I read that correctly. And just what is a decision bias? It could be thought of as that "still small voice" from your intuition that many think of as their "higher self" or even God. It is that "sense" we get when one choice "feels better" than another although we don't know why.

My thought about this phenomenon is that we learn many life-important lessons BEFORE we develop reasoning circuitry in our brains. That period of development we call infancy is also when we connect reward with context – the basis of decision bias. This could easily explain why some people feel inspired by a piece of music while another person is totally turned off by it. Context cues that trigger to reward – leading to a decision bias.

What happens when infancy is traumatic? What happens when contextual cues that would normally lead to reward (feelings of comfort and security) instead lead to pain and social exclusion? Or how about cues that would normally lead to pain and social exclusion instead lead to pleasure? What happens to later decision biases? I think it is obvious.

If you've been experiencing "twisted intuition" – that is, your sense of things or your "inner voice" or "inner guidance" seems to be off or too often incorrect – maybe it's time to reprogram. By reprogram, I mean, release the old subliminal programming and install new. If the old programming is left in place, any new programming will be based upon the old decision bias. In other words, the previous bias will affect any new

Some Common Thinking Errors and What to Do About Them

programming – making it nearly impossible to create a new underlying belief if it significantly differs from the previous one. You cannot place a new coat of paint over an old one and expect the new coat to stick to the wood underneath the old paint layer. You must first remove the old paint – and maybe even apply a primer coat to help the new paint coat stick better.

My Confirmation Bias

I like to think of myself as a very grounded, pragmatic person open to possibilities. I like evidence and supporting research that is non-biased. I used to think that double blind studies were the way to go because they seemed so objective – now I find that these, too, can be tainted and unreliable. I also like to try things out myself to get a more personal testimony of a process' efficacy – if it works well on me, I'll endorse it.

I have come to realize that scientific knowledge is not the same thing as understanding the scientific method. In the scientific method, one observes a phenomenon, then applies a possible theoretical hypothesis to that observation, tests the hypothesis in such a manner as to prove or disprove the hypothesis – making both results (proof or disproof) possible and viable, and then reevaluates in light of this new evidence.

The theoretical hypothesis is meant to be a notion – one that can be dismissed easily upon evidence to the contrary – weighing the evidence pro and con, choosing the most logical and reasonable explanation, regardless of what we previously believed. Testing must be as objective as possible and reproducible by others – making the testing process free from flukes and biases. Finally, analysis of the results of testing and reevaluation of the initial hypothesis must be done solely in light of the data extracted from objective testing – open equally to proof or disproof – free of political, social, economic, or other outside influences.

Then comes the rub – the "Confirmation Bias". The confirmation bias is defined as "sorting a body of data and selecting those that most confirm what we already believe, and ignoring or rationalizing away those that do not."

Our confirmation biases are based on teachings from our past – especially from our early childhood – from our earliest authorities – our parents! And where did they get their biases? Most likely from the same place you got yours – from their parents! This is how we instill and sustain our traditions, our superstitions, and our basic personal preferences – from our ancestors. Even when we are trained to do otherwise, we tend to fall back on our "DNA" – our family patterns of belief. It's even built into our physiology – our basic brain structure – and down into every cell.

Especially when it comes to issues relating to survival, we tend to confirm what we already believe and disregard or rationalize away the rest – our underlying subconscious belief being that our survival depends on keeping the status quo rather than releasing the old to investigate or consider something new and possibly better. Further, we will defend with our very lives our old "principles" based on those biases.

We tend to seek to prove to ourselves what we already believe rather than being truly open to surprise – no matter how pleasant the surprise may be. Further, we tend to taint our experiences to fit our biased world view. We simply cannot be truly objective. As humans, we carry within us the human trait of bias – and that bias is subconscious, deeply held, and strongly defended personally, culturally, and globally as a species. We taint every aspect of our lives with our own biases – it's natural and normal.

I have found that a healthy skepticism is useful in defeating confirmation bias. By healthy skepticism I mean questioning observations and conclusions in a framework of "Does this [observation / conclusion] confirm my preconception?" If so, then it's time to exercise some doubt. I tend to doubt my conclusions and observations. I wonder if I have perhaps tainted my observations and conclusions with my own beliefs and expectations.

My observation or conclusion may be correct. It could, however, be incorrect yet made correct to suit my bias. To test the veracity of my observations, I might, for example, ask others if they, too, experienced the same observation or came to the same conclusion. And, perhaps as important as confirmation from others, my openness to contrary observations and conclusions gives me additional information.

Perhaps the most useful to me is simply to give up my need to be right, proper, or justified. It's okay to make incorrect conclusions about observations. It's okay to be wrong. It's okay to use the words, "maybe", "perhaps", and "possibly" instead of "sure", "absolutely", and "certainly". "I wonder if…" opens further investigation, whereas, "It is…" seals the books. "It appears to me that…" and open ended questions like, "What could this mean?" tend to encourage truth-seeking and discourage bias-based certitude.

Some Common Thinking Errors and What to Do About Them

The LGBTQ Bias

Marginalized and dehumanized, one segment of the population have endured censorship, hatred, bigotry, and worse at the hands of their neighbors while contributing greatly to the overall sweetness and vitality of our human experience. Even research about them has been tainted by bias favoring heterosexual relationships as the "norm."

"The underlying assumption of research on LGBTQ (lesbian, gay, bi-sexual, transgender and queer) families has been premised on the idea that the children of gay and lesbian people will have unique challenges because of their parent's sexual orientation. LGBTQ people have had to establish that they are good parents by raising children who are hetero-sexual and gender-normative, i.e., not like them."

Family therapist and Social Work professor, Arlene Istar Lev says, "There is an assumption that the optimal outcome is to produce hetero-sexual children. I am questioning the heterosexism that pressures LGBTQ parents to prove their success as parents by producing hetero-sexual (read: normal) children. The research, steeped in heterosexist and heteronormative beliefs, assumes that if the children of LGBTQ people are gay or transgender themselves, it is a problem, a 'failure' revealing the ongoing bias against LGBTQ people."

Lev says, "Gay parents (just like heterosexual parents) may struggle with having gay or transgender children, in part because they identify with the obstacles their children will face, and in part because of the so-cietal pressure they feel to raise 'normal' (read: straight) children." Lev suggests that LGBTQ parents, as a minority that have been oppressed and marginalized, have a unique ability to accept and nurture their child-ren's emerging selves, if they see their own identity as an advantage, in-stead of something to be overcome. "If it is okay to be gay then it has to be okay for the children of gay people to be gay also."

Perhaps it's time to celebrate the unique qualities that gay and lesbian, bisexual and transgender parents bring to child-rearing. Instead of pres-suring gay parents to be "just like" straight parents, why not acknowl-edge and honor the differences - especially as they contribute to emo-tionally well adjusted, happy children (regardless of sexual orientation)? "We need to stop saying that being LGBTQ has no influence on children's identities; of course, it does. Maybe whatever it is that we are doing 'differently' is the reason our children are doing so well."

Perhaps it couldn't hurt to change our definition of "normal" or "successful" from "heterosexual" to "socially functional" or maybe just "happy".

Match and Lead

Mimicking a person can influence that person to adopt your point of view. In NLP, it's called "Match and Lead" – or "rapport".

In a series of experiments intended to demonstrate the power of mimicry, researchers discovered that, "A person who views someone else's snacking behavior will come to exhibit a similar snack selection pattern."[9]

"This suggests that preferences may shift as a result of unintentionally mimicking another person's consumption behavior."

In another experiment, researchers examined whether a person who is mimicked would come to like the person who mimicked them more than they would otherwise, and whether that would lead to a more positive response towards a product endorsed by the mimicker. Participants who had their posture, body angle, foot movements, and verbal patterns mimicked rated a new sports drink more positively and drank more of the sports drink than participants who were not mimicked. A separate experiment showed that the positive ratings and the amount consumed was even higher when the mimicker expressly stated that he or she was invested in the success of the product.

"This suggests that mimicry has the potential to be a valuable tool in interpersonal persuasion, particularly in cases where the motivations and persuasive intent of the mimicker are transparent," the researchers write. "So, even though consumers might try to resist a salesperson's pitch, being mimicked by that salesperson makes that pitch more impacting."

Match and lead. And here is the secret to matching and leading:

Match match match match

Match match match match

Match match match match

Match match match match

Maybe Lead

One must do quite a bit of matching in order to eventually maybe lead. I recommend testing through leading – just lead and see if they follow –

if they do, you're in; if they don't, then do more matching and try leading again later.

Most of us want to lead too soon – impatience has killed more than one sale.

The successful strategy for getting a customer, boss, contact, client, or spouse to buy your pitch is to ACT like them first (mimicking bodily movements and behaviors). This acting has the side benefit of helping you understand them better – increasing the chances that you will develop a mutually beneficial rapport.

Match, match, match, match, match…. maybe lead.

It's Never Over Until It's Over…

There was this fellow who wanted to demonstrate to the club pro that he could train a gorilla to play good golf. After many months of intense practice and training, the man felt that the gorilla was ready to take on the club pro.

He called the pro and set up a three-some. At the first tee, the club pro stepped up and hit a magnificent 250 yard drive right down the middle of the 500 yard first fairway. The pro huffed and snooted at the man and said in a rather condescending manner, "How about we place a little $1000 bet on this hole?"

The man felt pretty secure so he took the bet.

Then the gorilla stepped up to the tee. Thwack! The ball sailed out over the fairway and landed within three inches of the hole.

The pro dropped his shoulders and walked away dejected. Handing the man $1000, he asked in parting, "By the way, how is his putting?"

"Just like his driving - 500 yards every time!"

Moral of the story: The game is never over until it's over...

or...

Never bet against a gorilla trainer.

Some Common Thinking Errors and What to Do About Them

The Power of Positive Expectations

Three studies confirm that positive expectations tend to enhance heal-ing. So much so, in fact, that you can expect to recover as much as 3 times faster if you have positive recovery expectations.

On the other hand, if you have low expectations of recover, you can expect to heal as slowly as 4 times slower. That's a difference of 7 times – which means you can expect to heal as fast as seven times faster if you have positive expectations versus if you have negative expectations for recovery. That is significant!

What are we talking about? We're talking about one of my favorite subjects – the placebo (and its evil twin, the nocebo) effect – which states, in a nutshell, that you tend to get what you expect to get. Here are some interesting stats from the studies:

Linda Carroll, in the Canadian School of Public Health, looked at records of over 6,000 adults with traffic-related whiplash injuries. She found that those that had positive outlooks towards their recovery actual-ly recovered over three times faster than those who did not.

Dejan Ozegovic, also in the School of Public Health, looked at predic-tions around returning to work, using the same records. Positive return-to-work assumptions meant people rated themselves as "recovered" 42 per cent faster than those who had more negative expectations.

Lena Holm, a Swedish researcher who is working at the University of Alberta, found that those study participants in Sweden who had low ex-pectations of complete recovery were four times more likely to still feel symptoms of the injury six months later.

The researchers were surprised by the findings, which showed that the severity of the injury did not have an impact on the recovery times.

How fast do you think you'd recover from an injury if your physician were to tell you that you were unlikely to survive the night? This is the nocebo effect – that patients tend to fulfill their physician's negative ex-pectations for them. Are you willing to entrust your life to the *opinions* of an authoritative person like a physician? We have a bias that sets us up to believe authority figures. What can you do? Exercise some skepticism.

Some Common Thinking Errors and What to Do About Them

Power Questions

Using Questions to Empower You

Presuppositions are powerful suggestions that can be made in the course of ordinary conversation. Using presuppositions one can create influential questions that can open the mind and motivate one toward goal achievement.

Consider the difference between:

"I am going to buy a new house by the end of this year."

and

"How will I feel when I'm looking out the window of my new house later this year?"

Both are a kind of affirmation – one a goal statement and the other an evocative question based on an affirmation. The question evokes more emotion and motivation than does the statement. Why is that? Because we are built to answer questions.

Statements tend to evoke questions – like, "how can I do that?" Questions tend to evoke answers. It's what we do as humans.

Webster defines a presupposition as "an assumption that is taken for granted." When you assume a condition, it tends to be so – we call it expectation. I assume that to walk across the room, I will simply stand up, place one foot in front of the other, and walk. I take walking for granted. It is not a guarantee – I don't know that I won't suddenly fall or find that I cannot get up or walk. I take it for granted that it will happen just as I expect it to and I would be TERRIBLY disappointed if I could not walk. In fact, I might even be terrified if I suddenly could not walk. The assumption and expectation is great.

Building a question that contains a presupposition tends to make the question evocative in the direction of the presupposition. If your presupposition is an assumption of your goal already achieved – something you can then take for granted – you tend to open your mind to answers to your affirmation opposition thoughts.

Instead of "no, you can't" thinking, you will generate "this is why I can" thoughts. Later, you will generate "I knew I could" thoughts.

Some Common Thinking Errors and What to Do About Them

Here are a few presupposition laden example questions you can get started with:

- "Why am I so lucky?" (affirmation/presupposition: I am lucky – answers: all the reasons why)

- "What will I do first when I am at my ideal weight?" (affirmation/presup: I am at my ideal weight – answers: all the motivations to become thinner)

- "How happy will I be when I exceed my first million?" (affirmation/presup: I am a millionaire – answers: all the motivating feelings to take you over your goal)

- "Why do my clients love me so much?" (affirmation/presup: I am loved by my clients – answers: all the motivational reasons why you love yourself)

- "Why do I have such a successful and profitable practice?" (affirmation/presup: I am successful – answers: all the reasons why; reasons that motivate and support your goal)

- "Why am I so happy all the time?" (affirmation/presup: I am happy all the time – answers: all the motivational reasons why)

- "What new and exciting things will I discover about myself as I continue to enjoy my slender and healthy body?" (affirmation/presup: I am continuing to slim down – answers: all the motivational emotions necessary to sustain the weight reduction)

To build your own questions, just ask yourself, "What will life be like for me when I have already achieved my goal and I am taking it for granted?" Then make up questions about that state of being. Include your goal as a presupposed part of the question. For example, if your goal is to drop 30 pounds by Christmas, you might ask yourself first, what life would be like for you being 30 pounds lighter at Christmas time – which could take you to asking yourself something like, "What will Aunt Debbie say when she sees me 30 pounds lighter at Christmas time?"

The presupposition is that you will achieve your goal. The questions tend to evoke from you the motivation to achieve it. You don't have to worry about negative opposition from yourself because you are just asking a question – rather than giving an answer.

Some Common Thinking Errors and What to Do About Them

Ecology

There could be a time, however, when your question evokes a negative response. For example, if you asked yourself the question about Aunt Debbie and got a response from yourself, "She'd be so jealous she'd go into a deep depression;" you'd have an ecology problem. That is, by your achieving your goal, someone you care about will be injured or hurt or worse. If you get such a response from your question or any affirmation, it is time to reconsider your intent and your goal – because you will not achieve any goal that you believe will hurt someone you care about.

In such an instance, just rephrase your goal questions to evoke what feels good and warm to you – and avoids negative responses. Then, go work out your negative ecology with RET or another effective emotional clearing therapy until you can achieve your goal AND support those you love and care about.

Memory Access

Memories – such fleeting things sometimes. And yet, other memories seem to last and last – flush with details. Researchers at Duke University led by neuroscientist Roberto Cabeza, Ph.D. have discovered that information retrieved from memory is simultaneously processed in two specific regions of the brain, each of which focuses on a different aspect of a past event. The medial temporal lobe (MTL), located at the base of the brain, focuses on specific facts about the event. The frontal parietal network (FPN), located at the top of the brain, is more likely to process the global gist of the event.

What does this mean for us "ordinary folks?"

When you move your eyes, you tend to focus attention in your brain in an opposite direction. For example, when you look to the left, you tend to activate right hemisphere areas of your brain; when you look up, you tend to focus attention on lower brain areas, etc. It is as though you have a line-of-sight fulcrum inside your head with the fulcrum center-point in the very center of your brain (at eye level, of course). When you swing your gaze to the left, the other end of the fulcrum swings right, etc.

Consider this process to fully recall a memory:

First, look down, activating the FPN to get the gist of the memory. Cast your eyes side to side while looking downward to gain further information from the cerebral hemispheres associated with the FPN. When you feel ready to recall the details of that memory, swing your eyes upward and side-to-side. The upward gaze will tend to activate the MTL portion of your brain while the side-to-side action will tend to activate right and left hemispheres associated with the MTL.

Now, one more thing…

When you access a brain region, it wants something to DO. I recommend that you consider blinking – it's a simple and easy thing to do that creates huge fluctuations in light (from all to nothing and back). What you'll probably find is that by looking up and blinking, you'll activate the details-oriented MTL – and you'll stop blinking automatically as the details of a memory come to mind. Same goes for the FPN. My guess is that if someone were to be looking at your eyes while you do this, they'd see small but perceptible jumps in the size of your pupils as memory gist and details come to mind. For more exercises, see the next chapter.

Where you direct your eyes can make a difference in how you recall memories. Rapid eyelid blinking can stimulate emotions.

Some Common Thinking Errors and What to Do About Them

Exercises

Fall Out - Let gravity release any fear in an instant

So you have a fear and it's consuming your life. Maybe you're afraid to ask for that raise you deserve; or you're scared to death to face your spouse about his hurtful behavior; or maybe you're afraid you'll catch the Bird Flu. Whatever it is you're scared to death about, this little trick may help.

1. Imagine your fear – bring it up in your mind full force as best you can. If you prefer, you can actually come face-to-face with the object of your fear (at a comfortable, yet anxious distance – enough to scare you a little rather than a lot)
2. Notice – where in your body do you FEEL this fear? Take a physical inventory of your bodily sensations. This is the key – keep it physical.
3. Measure – apply the SUD scale to your sensations: 0 = no sensation ~ 10 = unbearable sensation.
4. Imagine a large tube or cylinder of water out in front of your body, filled with water to the level representative of the level of your SUD scale. Imagine how the tube of water feels (hot, cold, turbulent, soft, etc.); what it looks like, including color (tall, short, thin, fat, wooden, glass, metal, etc.); notice any sound it makes; make it as sensory real as you can in your imagination.
5. Now imagine you could reach out and remove the bottom of the tube and release ALL the water in a sudden rush out the bottom – letting gravity do its job. Whoosh!!
6. Repeat the entire process from step 1 above. You'll probably notice a substantial drop in SUD level. Continue this process until there is NO water in the tube at step 4.
7. Most important step – imagine you could PLUG UP the top and bottom of the tube so no water can reenter the tube.

Alternative 1- replace water with air pressure – like an air pressure gage. I've had clients who could easily imagine an air pressure gage releasing its air pressure with a WHOOSH sound – like a big sigh. Then, every

Some Common Thinking Errors and What to Do About Them

time a fear came up, they would make the sound and suddenly release all the "pressure".

Alternative 2 – imagine a toilet instead of a tube of water. Fill the toilet to the level of your SUD and at the appropriate time, flush the toilet... Make sure you place a lid on it and plug up its drain when you are done so it stays dry and empty in the future – until you want to use it, of course...

Personally, I prefer the water tube imagery because it depends upon gravity and I believe in gravity as a force of nature. It just is – without my intervention or assistance. I release the bottom of the tube and the water falls out of its own accord – no need for me to push it, pull it, or suck it out – it just FALLS OUT. And it's so easy to form some kind of cork to plug up top and bottom...

Some Common Thinking Errors and What to Do About Them

Taking Charge of Cause and Effect

Here is a simple exercise you can do yourself or with another to assist you in problem solving. Making use of cause and effect, you introduce an unknown (for now) resource into the equation that can help you get past your blocks to solving your own problem.

Exercise

Start with 5 sheets of paper. Write one of the following words on each sheet – Symptom, Cause, Outcome, Resource, Effect. These are your 5 anchors.

- *Symptom* means the set(s) of present behaviors or feelings that reflect the problem.

- *Cause* means the cause of the problem, as you think it is/was.

- *Outcome* is the outcome that you want/will have when this is no longer a problem.

- *Resource* is the resource (what it will take to correct the problem) that escapes you, for now.

- *Effect* is the effect that the change will have on you.

Then…

1. Think of a problem you are trying to solve

2. On the floor, lay out your four spatial anchors (papers with the words you made before) in a sequence representing the cause, symptom, outcome and effect related to the problem. Keep them close enough so you can step from one to another. Set the Resource anchor pad separately like this:

   < -------------------[Resource]---------------------->

   [Cause] → [Symptom] → [Outcome] → [Effect]

3. Physically step on each paper one at a time in order (cause, symptom, outcome, effect), and associate into the experience an internal state related to each anchor point. Pay attention to the pattern of movement associated with each location, intensifying it a little to help build your sense of the physiology asso-

Some Common Thinking Errors and What to Do About Them

ciated with each element (notice how your body moves, feels, and senses at each point – if you feel like your body wants to jump up and down and throw a fit, do it, right there; if you have an itch, scratch it; if your body gets hot, notice it).

4. Starting at the cause anchor, walk slowly through the entire sequence – notice how you feel at each point. Repeat this process several times until there is a sense of a single movement from cause to effect.

5. Step on the Resource paper, and let your mind and body lead you to a special movement representing the appropriate RESOURCE to bring into the sequence. This is the same process as in step 3. Intensify this movement.

6. Starting in the cause location, incorporate the resource movement into the other movement associated with that location. Walk through the other locations, or anchors, adding the resource movement until you have reached the effect anchor.

7. Repeat the movement through cause, symptom, outcome and effect until you have transformed it into a kind of dance.

Variation for Rapid Eye Technicians:

Use the exercise with the Circle of Creation Walk – do it yourself or with a client. Place the "Connection to God" pad in the center of the circle (or, for clients who don't care to use "God" or "Source", create a pad called "Ultimate Resource" instead). Repeat the above exercise on each pad of the Walk, in proper sequence from Environment to Spirit – creating a body movement for each pad.

Make sure to create a movement or "dance" on the "Connection to God" or "Ultimate Resource" pad – and add that dance to the other pads in reverse order back to the "Environment" pad (the beginning) – each pad's new dance adding to the overall dance. Before they step off the Environment pad prepare them to dance the ENTIRE dance in their own personal space – a new energy circle they create when they step off the Environment pad.

Treat this step-off area like you would an energy circle – put all the new positive feelings, etc., gained from the walk into the circle – plus the "dance". Then jump into the new energy circle and instead of pulling the energy up like clothing, DANCE your DANCE – full out!! (note to Technician: you may need to

Some Common Thinking Errors and What to Do About Them

step back a bit from your client for this part) If a song comes to mind, sing it out loud as best you can to support your dance.

This dance will imprint your resourceful state into your cells in a body-centric way. Remind your client (or yourself if doing this yourself) that your resourceful state will follow you when you leave this session – and return to you whenever you dance your dance or think of dancing your dance...

When faced with challenges about your goal in the future, just start dancing!

Some Common Thinking Errors and What to Do About Them

The Creation Mantra

I also like the idea of saying to myself (maybe as a mantra), "I am experiencing exactly what I want to experience right now or I'd be experiencing something else. I am doing exactly what I most want to do right now or I'd be doing something else. I have exactly what I want to have right now or I'd have something else." (BE-DO-HAVE)

I think that when you adopt this as a personal truth, you tend to take responsibility for your life and magical things start to happen. For one, when you are the responsible party, you have the power to make changes – not because you don't like what you have; rather, because you love what you have and want to experience something else you love.

If you want to make a substantial change in your life, consider taking responsibility for your life – acknowledge that you are, do, and have what you currently experience because you want to.

How you feel about what you experience is your payoff. Embrace your payoff – you love it, after all – and you've gone to some effort and energy to achieve it. Investigate what other payoffs you might enjoy just as much and begin embracing that instead.

You might also enjoy achieving your current payoff in a different manner. Like the kid in the sandbox making a sand castle, you can play with your design as much as you wish until you get it "just right" – that is, you experience sufficient sensational payoff.

Connecting with Your Values

Reflecting on your values can help you feel less defensive and more connecting.

Want to feel less defensive? Want to feel more loving and kind? Want to better connect with others?

Then you would benefit from a short exercise you can do any time. A new study published in the July issue of Psychological Science, a journal of the Association for Psychological Science, found that writing about important values makes people feel loving and connected, and that these other-directed feelings account for reduced defensiveness.

"These studies raise the prospect that reminding people what they love or care about may enable them to transcend the self and may foster learning under difficult circumstances," Jennifer Crocker and Yu Niiya from the University of Michigan and Dominik Mischkowski from the University of Konstanz, the study authors explain.

The exercise is simple:

Take 10 minutes and write about something you care about – a value. For example, you could write about your feelings about your home and why it is important to you. You might choose to write about your marriage or your pet or your friends or your most prized possession or even a more esoteric value like why you feel as you do about your religion. Each of these subjects would elicit your values and help you connect with that part of you that transcends pettiness and defensiveness.

Got a big test or job interview coming up? Do the exercise just before you take the test or face the interviewer.

Maybe you have little time – the boss has called you into her office and you have that feeling it isn't going to be about a raise – as you walk toward her office, rather than ruminating on why your boss might want to "chat" with you, reflect instead upon your most cherished values (what is important in life for you and why). You'll connect better with the boss and feel less defensive overall. And probably set up the energy of a successful and rewarding encounter – and maybe turn a chewing out into a raise after all!

Some Common Thinking Errors and What to Do About Them

The Mystery Story Worth Reading

I'm less than halfway though my life story and it's so intensely interesting that I can't take my attention off it.

I'm a real fan of mystery movies. I love Perry Mason and Philip Marlowe. I especially love the "whodunit" type stories. They entertain me all the way to the end because I want to try to figure out whodonit before they show me. Sometimes I actually get it right – and I congratulate myself for it, too. I'm less than halfway though my life story and it's so intensely interesting that I can't take my attention off it. So many characters, so many story twists, so much action and intrigue – thoroughly entertaining. I'm enjoying it so much, I don't want it to end.

What has happened in your life to give it pizzazz? I wonder what would happen with you if you suddenly chose to view your life from the perspective of an intriguing movie – one you would pay top dollar to see – a real blockbuster.

Why do you go see the movies you do now? What kind of movie draws your attention? What would happen if you chose to consider your own life as that kind of story?

It doesn't help to look at your life in the same way that disinterests you – you may have already done that. If you are not thoroughly entertained with the story now, why would you suddenly be interested in viewing it from the same perspective you did before? With a new perspective, you may find that you really like your life story – maybe find that it is well worth the price of admission.

Can you recall a movie you really loved – maybe one you went to see more than once? Remember it well – see it, hear it, maybe even smell the popcorn you ate… Now, quite suddenly, apply that interest to your life. Tell yourself inside that the movie you really loved is the movie of your life.

It's not the life you live that makes the difference – it's how much you like the life you live that matters. And that level of interest is entirely your choice. You choose how much you enjoy the movies you view. You can choose how much you enjoy your own live movie. You don't have to rewrite it – just re-evaluate how well you like it. Then choose to enjoy it thoroughly. It's much easier than you might imagine.

Some Common Thinking Errors and What to Do About Them

Once you enjoy the story, the story becomes that much more enjoyable. Everything works as smoothly as a slide downhill.

My Inner Child just loves stories!

Some Common Thinking Errors and What to Do About Them

What and How

Perhaps you already know that you have two hemispheres to your cortex. Although each hemisphere seems to govern certain types of thought patterns, they communicate with each other to such a degree that it is hard to discern their separate functions. However, by taking charge of those hemispheres you can take charge of your mood, your choices, and your communications – making it easier for you to function, achieve goals, study, interact, and communicate with yourself and others.

You don't need to be a neurosurgeon or brain specialist to take charge of your brain. Just as you don't have to understand how a computer works to make it work for you, you can obtain substantial benefit from your brain without having to understand how it works. You just need the right "software" a program you can run. And just as with your computer's software, which program you run and what you input into the program can make quite a difference in the output you get.

For example, if I wish to print a page of text from my computer, I would first fire up my computer and select my word processor to input the text using my keyboard. Then I'd save the resulting text in a file – it's always a good idea to back up your work. I'd then hit my "print" key or select print from the menu of my program and send the resulting bits and bytes to my connected printer.

Using the right hardware and software, I got a result that matched my desire – to print out a copy of my ideas.

I did not have to know how my computer did what I asked it to do. All I had to do was become familiar enough with the software to operate it. I didn't have to know how my monitor or printer works in order to get my page printed. I just hit the "print" key.

Below is a simple little "utility" program for your brain that utilizes both hemispheres. This little program or exercise is based on Rapid Eye Technology (RET). The end result of this exercise is information gathering – to help you make more useful choices.

1. Look slightly to the left of center and slightly above horizontal and ask yourself, "What do I want?" (maybe there is some goal or problem troubling you) Keep your answer simple – "I want to

Some Common Thinking Errors and What to Do About Them

improve my grade in math class by one grade…" – remember to keep things realistic…

2. Look slightly to the right and slightly below horizontal and ask yourself, "How do I feel about what I want?" Notice what your body says by way of sensations – just note them, we'll use these later.

3. Look to the left and slightly below horizontal and ask yourself, "Why do I want this?" Again, note how your body feels.

4. Look slightly to the right and slightly above horizontal and ask yourself, "When have I felt like this (wanting whatever it is you want) before?" While looking in this area consider as many times as will pop into your mind of times you remember feeling like you do now as you consider your desired outcome.

5. Blink hard three times – use your whole face to blink closed HARD – open – close HARD- open – closed HARD – open.

6. Sigh deeply three times.

7. Let your mind go by simply closing your eyes and letting the ideas flow.

8. Move your body – in whatever motion feels "right" to you. The movement energizes your brain and gets your chemicals in alignment with your desire.

9. Most important – take action! Now that you have some ideas, do something constructive toward achieving what you want.

Some Common Thinking Errors and What to Do About Them

Make Cause and Effect Work for You

Throughout your life you've been conditioned and conditioned yourself to believe in certain cause and effect relationships. Some of your cause-effect relationships may be faulty, however, because you formed in your mind some of those cause-effect relationships at times when you were too young, too ignorant, too traumatized, and/or too inexperienced to adequately evaluate the evidence at hand.

With practice, you've perfected your cause and effect relationships to such an extent that they have become automatic – so much so that you simply accept them as truth without question. Further, you tend to apply the "rules" of those relationships to later similar events. For example, the rule that "men cannot be trusted" because (cause-effect) one molested me as a child – taints all future encounters – setting up romantic interludes for failure before they even start. And there's the first rub – your faulty cause-effect relationships have become so automatic you no longer question them – in fact, you may indeed be completely unaware of many of them.

As physicists have discovered, there is no way to know ALL the possible outcomes of any given action. Probability dictates that a specific outcome may be far more likely than another. Still, there is no way to absolutely know for sure that a specific outcome (effect) will occur due to a specific action (cause). Conversely, it is impossible to determine with absolute surety a cause from an effect – there are just too many variables involved. That is why science deals in probabilities rather than certainties – cause and effect is simply impossible to connect with absolute surety. And there's the second rub – you cannot with surety determine cause from effect or effect from cause.

And then there is the third rub – the fact that we as humans love to be right. In short, we are willing to ascribe any cause to any effect if we feel it makes us right, proper, or justified. We can even convince ourselves that these cause-effect relationships are true no matter how absurd or unrealistic they may be. We're even willing, in most cases, to defend our cause-effect relationships against an onslaught of contradicting evidence. Justification gives us permission to lie, cheat, steal, make war, and worse in the name of being right. God is still God (metaphorically) no matter how strong the evidence against the concept. Rightness is more important that truth.

Some Common Thinking Errors and What to Do About Them

Turning Cause and Effect on Its Head

The keyword here is the word "because" – in English the word "because" joins together our cause-effect relationships. Something is so BECAUSE something else is so. Someone did something BECAUSE something else happened. Something will happen BECAUSE something else happened. Because, because, because… In this series of exercises, you will be challenging your most treasured and sacred cause-effect relationships so they become exposed to your conscious awareness and no longer as automatic.

Exercise 1 – Real Effect, Unrelated Cause

Every time you hear yourself say or think the word "because" – in your mind create a nonsense joiner. A joiner is the ending to a sentence – the part that comes after the word, "because." For example, if I were to normally say, "I'm going out tonight because I deserve it." Instead I might say something like, "I'm going out tonight because that door is open." – completely separating cause from effect. With practice this fun and often comical game can become a real powerful therapy all by itself.

Exercise 2 – Specific Real Negative Effect, Unrelated Absurd Cause

Every time you notice that you are doing something that does not support your goals tell yourself in your mind, "I'm [doing this real action] because [absurd description of something impossible]." For example, "I'm eating this cake because gorillas are purple." In this exercise your job is to make the joiner absolutely as absurd and impossible as you can. Get ridiculous with this exercise – only use it when you have done something you know you should not have done.

Exercise 3 – Specific Real Positive Effect, Unrelated Real Material Cause

Every time you notice that you have done something that supports your goals – like exercising – tell yourself in your mind, "I did that because I have [some item in your world]." For example, if you are seeking to drop

Some Common Thinking Errors and What to Do About Them

some pounds and you just came in after exercising, you might say to yourself, "I just exercised because there is a window in my kitchen." In this exercise your job is to create a joiner that is true yet not related at all to the behavior (what does a kitchen window have to do with you exercising, for example). Remember – do this exercise ONLY for those times when you notice that you are doing what will support your new body image.

To reinforce and energize this series of exercises you can document your experiences in a journal. The overall goal of these exercises is to get you to pay attention to your cause-effect relationships – to respond to them – and in the end, challenge them. Don't let them just "be" – check your "evidence" against adult reason. Just because someone hurt you when you were a child does not necessarily mean they or someone else is going to hurt you now.

What More Can You Do?

Objectify your evidence – Pretend you are an alien, unfamiliar with our culture. How would such an alien look at your evidence? **Forgive** - Acknowledge that you goofed when you made your "because" truth. It happens all the time in humans. So, you were human! So what?! Move on!

Become a skeptic – You can do it. Challenge your becauses each time you hear or recognize them. Here's some ideas:

- Ask yourself, "Is this really true?" – "Do I really know this is true?" – "Can I know this is really true?"

- Ask yourself, "Who would I be without this truth?"

- Ask yourself, "What OTHER reasons could there be?" – "If this were not true, what ELSE could be true instead?"

- Ask yourself, "Where could I have gotten THAT idea?" – "Who taught me to believe that?" (and when?)

Identify which – Note whether you are attempting to make yourself right, justified, or proper (to fit in with your peers). It's okay to be right – and we tend to feel better when we feel our actions are justified – it's when being right or justified means everything that we can have a problem. It's how wars erupt.

Take charge – Your cause-effect relationships are yours, so own them. Only the owner of a belief can change it. When you notice a cause-effect relationship getting in your way, own it! Then manipulate it using the exercises above – and rewrite it to suit your present situation and environment.

Cleaning the Gene Pool – An Imagery

Relax yourself as though your body were a rag doll – floppy and limp. Allow your breathing to assist you to relax every muscle. Let every thought simply pass through you like a moving stream. (pause) In time, you find yourself wanting to follow the stream... (pause) ...gently down the hill... down... down... down... until... at last... you come to... the lowest point... at the bottom... of the stream...

Imagine you are sitting comfortably beside a large pool of water. As the image of it comes to you, please describe it... (Notice the description for use in the rest of this imagery)

Now notice a person walking up to you. As you look up, you realize that this person is the future adult growing within you now. This person has a smile on their face and thanks in their heart for the work you have done in their behalf. There is an immediate feeling of love and affection between you that feels like it has gone on forever.

Now the two of you are sitting together looking over the pool. You suddenly realize that the pool you are looking over is your own gene pool and it needs some serious cleaning! You notice, too, that your companion is superbly fit and strong, clean, and easily able and willing to assist you in cleaning the pool.

Magically, there appear the tools and implements for cleaning. Together, you begin to clean; scrubbing the pool and purifying the water; and as you do, you see the shapes of humans rising out of the water, sparklingly clean, to join you in cleaning; you realize that these are your family members, and ancestors.

Together you join to clean the pool. The more you clean, the more clean people rise up out of the water to assist you. The pool begins to get clean very fast. Soon, you realize that the pool is totally clean with beautiful, clean people seated around the pool.

Everyone is clean of all their wounds, all their hurtful beliefs and emotions, all their contributions to the gene pool are now washed clean. Now that the gene pool is clean and clear, you all have a desire to swim in the clear, clean water.

Feel the water cool your body and strengthen it as you swim out into the gene pool. Feel the clear, clean, sparkling energy massage, nurture,

Some Common Thinking Errors and What to Do About Them

and vitalize all your bodies. You might notice how you all begin to merge together in the soft, sweet water, into a sense of generational one-ness.

Because of this nurturing pool of support, your mind can float out ahead in time and imagine the distant future with generations of healthy and well-balanced families based on your clear and clean gene pool.

(pause)

Let yourself integrate all the clear and clean genetic information brought together for you during this experience into every cell of your being – reminding each cell of its genetic inheritance – a clear and clean gene pool.

Imagine yourself climbing up out of the water onto the land. Notice how strong and capable you now feel. Every cell in your body is now infused with a genetic purpose and will. Wellness and strength fill every layer and level of your being. Breathe the breath of life into every cell. (Deep breath)

As you come fully present, know that your mind and body are now aligned with your genetic creational blueprint – free and clear – like a shiny new coin. You carry with you that clear clean water you swam in just moments ago – it surrounds every cell.

You may now more fully appreciate the taste of clean water – and with every drink of clear water you take, your mind will flash back on this experience and remind every cell of its genetic purpose and will. Each time you see a body of water, your mind will refresh its memory of your clean gene pool and how good it feels to swim in it.

It's time now to come fully present. Take a deep breath and allow your consciousness to come fully present into the room with me now. Gently open your eyes when you are ready.

Some Common Thinking Errors and What to Do About Them

Rapid Eye Yoga for Performance Boost

It was 1991. Twelve shooters remained at the firing line, their scores too low to pass the Army National Guard weapons qualifications requirement. All twelve shooters were stressed to the max. If they failed the test, they lost their jobs. For them it had come down to this one moment – pass or fail.

The stress was palpable as the shooters stepped up to the firing line with their M-16 for their "last chance". Fortunately for them, I was in charge of that firing line that day. I told the shooters to add just one simple action to their shooting process. I instructed them to simply cast their eyes several times from side to side and then up and down as far and as fast as they could move their eyes, then shut them very hard and open again three times and then make a big sigh – then shoot.

Each shooter had 60 seconds to fire 20 rounds from each of 5 positions – 100 shots in roughly 5 minutes. Each had to hit a tiny silhouette marked on a target 100 meters away. To pass, each had to hit the target at least 60 times (60%). Every shooter had previously missed that minimum requirement and this was their "last chance" to qualify.

This time, as each shooter took their firing position, they added the eye movement and breathing technique to their process just before firing their weapon. And this time, each hit the target more than 80 times, the best shooter hitting the target 95 times – missing only 5 times when before he had missed at least 40 times. ALL shooters passed the test that day – and breathed a sigh of relief!

After that incident, I was called upon several more times to perform the same "miracle". Most of those to whom I taught this simple technique remembered it and never again needed coaching.

Ever found yourself "up against the wall" and stressed to the max? Perhaps you have a final exam you must pass or a competition you fret over. Whatever the reason for the performance anxiety-laden stress, the simple technique of rapidly moving your eyes back and forth several times, moving them up and down several times, blinking as hard as you can three times and then breathing deeply in a deep sigh, can both instantly reduce stress levels and help you perform better in that moment.

Some Common Thinking Errors and What to Do About Them

When it comes to performance, your stressed mind will produce fight or flight chemicals in your body – like cortisol. Unfortunately, cortisol and other stress chemicals tend to shut down the parts of the body necessary for peak performance – like cognitive thinking, intuition, and muscular coordination – in favor of brute force to either escape or fight a predator. When it comes to performance tests like shooting, a clear and well-functioning mind will win out over brute force every time.

The experience at the firing range taught me valuable lessons about stress and how a simple technique can make all the difference. Want to quickly double your reading speed and comprehension – almost instantly? Try this: just before you engage in reading, cast your eyes to their peripheries as quickly as you can – laterally and vertically – several times – until it begins to feel uncomfortable. Then blink hard three to five times and sigh deeply afterward. Then read. You'll be amazed at how much faster you can comprehend each page you read. And all you did was prepare your mind with a simple physical process – a little "rapid eye yoga".

Some Common Thinking Errors and What to Do About Them

Using Your Whole Brain

There are obvious advantages to using both hemispheres when addressing a goal or project. When both "people" in your head work together on a common goal, magical things tend to happen. The reason those magical things don't happen more often may be because your brains are in conflict with each other. Bringing them together in a common direction may be all you need to do to get things moving in your life – moving in the direction of your goals.

Quite basically, you have one brain hemisphere that thinks in a linear fashion and is great for organization. The other is great for spatial, non-concrete thinking – creativity. To avoid total confusion, we humans will assign one brain hemisphere or the other to be dominant for any given task. Usually the dominant one is the one that was dominant the last time you did the task – not because it is better suited to the task, but purely by the luck of the draw – that was the one that happened to be dominant at that time.

That's pretty haphazard if you ask me.

What I'm writing about here is brain dominance. Contrary to what I was taught in college, we are not left or right brain dominant all the time. In other words, you are not "left brain dominant" or "right brain dominant." Every two to three hours our brains subtly shift from right dominance to left dominance and back again.

The shift is very subtle and you probably won't notice the shift. You might notice the shift if you are currently in your right brain dominance and suddenly are faced with a left brain task. Your brain will shift dominance to accommodate the task – according to the blueprint of the last time you did the task – or perhaps you've done the task repeatedly using that brain hemisphere and now have a habit of it – like tying your shoes or reading the Sunday comics.

Shifting brain dominance at will can give you more control and bring your strongest assets to bear on whatever task you may be faced with at the time. Rather than relying upon the haphazard approach previously employed in which brain dominance for a task relied upon a chance occurrence in your past, we can now take charge of our own brain dominance and use that dominance to enhance our life experiences.

Some Common Thinking Errors and What to Do About Them

Manually change brain dominance

Imagine a fulcrum (a compass is a fulcrum) in which the center of the fulcrum is in the center of your brain (see illustration on the next page).

As you imagine swinging the fulcrum to the left in front of you, the rear of the fulcrum will swing to the right rear. To change brain dominance at will, simply imagine the fulcrum swinging from one side in front of you to the other side - with a corresponding opposite effect to the rear.

You do not have to move your eyes or head or body in any way. Simply imagine the fulcrum shifting from side to side with the opposite effect to the rear.

This exercise will shift your underlying attention and focus to one side from the other. For example, as you begin to read, imagine shifting the fulcrum in your head to the other side and see if reading becomes any easier - or that you begin to comprehend the material any better - or both.

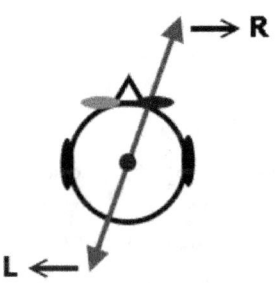

Viewed from above, the dot in the middle represents the fulcrum point.

Experiment with other tasks to see how things go for you. For most projects or activities, shifting back and forth from one side to the other and then back again - slowly - will cause additional brain assets to come into focus for a short time - usually long enough to engage them. It will also cause the Corpus Callosum* to communicate quicker and more often between brain hemispheres - balancing out your resources and compelling images as you go along. [10]

The Corpus Callosum is a brain structure that connects right and left hemispheres of the cerebral cortex.

Some Common Thinking Errors and What to Do About Them

Rapid Switching

You can either learn or remember. Researchers at Duke University[11] used functional magnetic resonance imagery (fMRI) to demonstrate this competition in a group of college age adults. Their evidence is compelling. Many psychological studies have also shown that you can either listen for new information or consider your response to that information (remembering similar past events). One or the other – not both simultaneously.

New OR old rather than new AND old. You can either listen to your partner's complaint OR search your memory for a snappy comeback – not both simultaneously.

The problem, of course, arises when the switch is turned to focus the brain on remembering when learning is indicated – or visa versa. Too many times I've come back with a response to my wife's information that was completely off or indicated that I was not intent or focused on what she was saying. Rather, I was "remembering" similar information – and probably getting side-tracked by a mind tangent – rather than "learning" I was "remembering". Oops!

"I can do that, daddy!" My father heard these words often from me as a kid – especially after a short demonstration of a skill he was trying to teach me. He'd invariably turn the task over to me whereupon the task would get horribly bungled because I had no clue what I was doing. I was remembering a similar task rather than paying attention to the lesson at hand. The switch was in the wrong position. Oops!

How does one manually turn the switch from one state to the other? Certainly this could be a valuable skill for many tasks including academic learning, attending to the needs of a partner, or learning how to operate equipment.

As learning new concepts mostly involves the right hemisphere while attending to memories is more concentrated in the left hemisphere, learning to manually switch brain dominance at will could assist one in "focusing" on the proper task at the proper time.

A simple method for manually switching from Remembering to Learning and back again

Just as in the previous exercise, imagine a spot in the very center of your cortex (upper brain). This will be the pivot point.

Next imagine a laser light beam that originates in the distance to your right, through your right eye and pivot point, ending up on the left rear wall of your brain. You might look slightly toward the right of center to heighten the effect. Imagine the entire line like a light beam.

This will tend to activate LEFT brain dominance – REMEMBERING.

To switch to learning, simply reverse the laser beam origin point to the left side of center – through the eye and the pivot point – to the right rear wall of the brain. Imagine the entire line like a light beam.

This will tend to activate RIGHT brain dominance – LEARNING

At any moment you find yourself remembering when you want to be learning, just flash on the image of a laser beam from the LEFT side entering your eye, passing through the pivot point in the center of your brain, and illuminating the RIGHT rear wall of your brain.

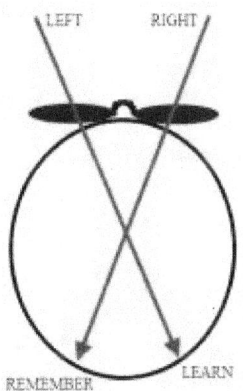

Imagine a laser light beam through the center of your brain.

Sure, doing the imagery is using memory (you must remember the imagery to use it). However, flashing on the image of the entire laser light beam will tend to jump you off remembering and back into learning.

With practice, you can use an anchoring technique[12] to invoke the imagery. For example, whenever you imagine the laser beam from the left side, you might wiggle your left index finger in a certain way. Over time practicing associating the wiggling of your left index finger with the image of the laser beam from the left side, your brain will instantly evoke the learning mode whenever you wiggle your left index finger. The same could be done on the right side for remembering – a handy tool when you get out of class and need to find your car in the parking lot…

Some Common Thinking Errors and What to Do About Them

Need to remember a license plate number or a sequence of numbers or a math table or spelling list? Laser beam from the RIGHT! Need to understand that new concept in your physics or math class? Laser beam from the LEFT! Need to connect heart to heart with your spouse? Laser LEFT! Then RIGHT! First, left to "hear" him/her with intent to understand and learn; then right to store the new information and to associate with memories of sweetness, gentleness, kindness, and love. Respond from these memories. Then switch back left to "hear" the lesson.

Help Your Memory by Moving Your Eyes[13]

Moving your eyes horizontally, from side-to-side, for about 30 seconds may be all it takes to give your memory a boost, according to researchers from Manchester Metropolitan University in England.

After hearing a list of words, the study found that those who moved their eyes side-to-side for 30 seconds correctly remembered more than 10 percent more words, and falsely recognized about 15 percent fewer "lure" words, compared to those who moved their eyes up and down or did nothing.

Why would moving your eyes influence your memory?

The researchers suspect it's because the horizontal eye movements cause the two hemispheres of the brain to interact more, and communication between the left and right brain hemispheres is known to help us remember certain things.

The researchers aren't sure whether the eye movements will help people in their daily lives ... but it's certainly worth a try the next time you've misplaced your keys or forgotten your grocery list at home!

Making It Happen in Writing!

You've probably heard and seen them all – sure-fire ways to manifest what you want. Here's a rather simple method that takes your ideas out of your head and gives them a head-start (so to speak) by manifesting your goals in writing first. This starting point seems to set them up for manifestation and is a lot of fun to boot.

Some years ago, Ranae Johnson, the originator of Rapid Eye Technology, kept a shoe box in which we placed such papers – like a wish list. I don't know what happened to the box. I do know what happened to my life – it took off in the directions I wrote about – BIG TIME.

Write out what you want on a piece of paper:

- How much you want it.
- When you want it.
- Then elicit your criteria for why it's important to get all this good stuff.

The next part is essential – *sign the piece of paper*. You have a contract with yourself now! You're committed. Now your unconscious and conscious can align and do everything possible to make it happen.

Do this for:

- 1-month outcome
- 3-month outcome
- 6-month outcome

Include these categories:

- Financial (minimum earnings)
- Career (change of position or accomplishments)
- Health (weight, food, exercise, healing)
- Spiritual (growth, wisdom, breakthroughs)
- Social (friends, outings, hobbies, activities)

Some Common Thinking Errors and What to Do About Them

Now set the paper aside somewhere safe and get busy putting your plans into action. Action is the key - writing your goals means nothing if you don't back it up with action.

A few months from now, you'll find that paper and delight in what has happened.

The key to making it work, however, is urgency – DO IT NOW. Stop reading this, get a piece of paper and a pen, and do this exercise RIGHT NOW! Don't wait to do it later when it's more convenient (because it never will be). Don't figure that you'll get around to it (because you never will). This is in your face RIGHT NOW for a reason. RIGHT NOW is the time for you to do this and get the magic started for you – RIGHT NOW!

Let me help you with one category (say, Financial):

What do you want? Write it down here:

How much do you want it? (A whole lot, I hope!) Write it:

Why is this important to you? Write it down here:

At one month, I expect to see:

At three months, I expect to see:

At six months, I expect to see:

(Repeat for the other categories – Career, Health, Spiritual, and Social)

Some Common Thinking Errors and What to Do About Them

Not Exercises

The word "not" can activate possibility thinking - breaking up writer's block, reenergizing brain storming sessions, sparking new and innovative thinking, and much more.

Process 1 - Untying your own nots

Use this process when you are stuck in a rut, wanting to make a quick incremental (small) life change - like making more money or improving your golf game.

1) Think about what is stuck or not moving in your life - what you want to change. Speak it out loud to yourself - "I am stuck doing [whatever]." Include whatever "and" statements make it real to you. For example, "I'm stuck being poor and I can never make enough to pay my bills." Just say it the way you mean it.

2) Measure the level of disturbance this problem feels to you on a scale of 0-10 with ten being so disturbing that it consumes you and zero meaning it does not disturb you at all.

3) Cover one eye with the palm of your hand - keep both eyes open.

4) Say out loud to yourself the following slowly (pause between each statement and think about it for 5 seconds)

    a) I am stuck. <pause 5 seconds> (ex: "I am stuck being poor.")

    b) I am not stuck. <pause 5 seconds> (ex: "I am not stuck being poor.")

    c) I am not not stuck. <pause 5 seconds> (ex: "I am not not stuck being poor.")

5) Cover the other eye and repeat the previous step

6) Re-measure level of disturbance.

    a) If you feel more disturbed and less capable of resolving the issue, consider getting professional assistance from a qualified therapist.

b) If the level remains about the same, consider repeating the exercise with one of the variations listed at the end of this set of exercises (see page 140).

c) If the level drops significantly, repeat the exercise and add substance to it (example: "I am stuck and feel pressured…")

d) *Note: the level of disturbance may never drop to zero. The aim of this exercise is to lower the level to a point where you feel capable of doing constructive action aimed at resolving the issue.*

7) Pause for a moment and explore this statement: "If I were not stuck, what would I be?"

Process 2 - Getting out of your own way

Use this process of nots to stop undermining your own efforts. Maybe you've noticed over time a pattern of sabotage - undermining your own efforts. Usually you can put it into words like, "Every time I try to [blank], I [blank]" The first blank is filled in with your desired goal and the second with the way you sabotage yourself. For example, "Every time I try to ask for a raise, I stumble over my words and look like an idiot."

Think about the way you sabotage your own efforts - maybe make a list of the ways you've seen yourself do it.

1) Focus your attention on one way you sabotage your efforts.

2) Measure the level of disturbance this problem is to you on a scale of 0-10 with ten being so disturbing that it consumes you and zero meaning it does not disturb you at all.

3) Cover one eye with the palm of your hand - keep both eyes open.

4) Say out loud to yourself the following slowly (pause between each statement and think about it for 5 seconds)

a) I am [sabotage behavior]. <pause 5 seconds> (ex: "I am stumbling over my words.")

b) I am not [sabotage behavior]. <pause 5 seconds> (ex: "I am not stumbling over my words.")

Some Common Thinking Errors and What to Do About Them

   c) I am not not [sabotage behavior]. <pause 5 seconds> (ex: "I am not not stumbling over my words.")

5) Cover the other eye and repeat the previous step

6) Pause for a moment and explore this statement: "If I were not sabotaging my own efforts, what would I be doing?"

7) Repeat from step 2 with a new way you sabotage your efforts.

8) Re-measure level of disturbance.

   a) If you feel more disturbed and less capable of resolving the issue, consider getting professional assistance from a qualified therapist.

   b) If the level remains about the same, consider repeating the exercise with one of the variations listed at the end of this set of exercises (see page 140).

   c) If the level drops significantly, repeat the exercise and add substance to it (example: "I am stuck and feel pressured...")

   d) *Note: the level of disturbance may never drop to zero. The aim of this exercise is to lower the level to a point where you feel capable of doing constructive action aimed at resolving the issue.*

9) Continue the whole process until you have run out of ways you sabotage yourself.

Process 3 - Increasing ability and skill

Use this process to improve your game, make more sales, enrich your life. Maybe you are looking for a way to get an edge or improve what you are already doing well. This might look like the statement, "If I didn't [blank], I could [blank]." The first blank would be filled in with what keeps you from your goal and the second with your goal. For example, "If I didn't triple putt every hole, I could beat par for the course."

1) Think about what it is that keeps you from doing better.

2) Measure the level of disturbance this problem is to you on a scale of 0-10 with ten being so disturbing that it consumes you and zero meaning it does not disturb you at all.

3) Cover one eye with the palm of your hand - keep both eyes open.

4) Say out loud to yourself the following slowly (pause between each statement and think about it for 5 seconds)

   a) I am doing [what keeps you from doing better]. <pause 5 seconds> (ex: "I am triple putting every hole.")

   b) I am not doing [what keeps you from doing better]. <pause 5 seconds> (ex: "I am not triple putting every hole.")

   c) I am not not doing [what keeps you from doing better]. <pause 5 seconds> (ex: "I am not not triple putting every hole.")

5) Cover the other eye and repeat the previous step.

6) Re-measure level of disturbance.

   a) If you feel more disturbed and less capable of resolving the issue, consider getting professional assistance from a qualified therapist.

   b) If the level remains about the same, consider repeating the exercise with one of the variations listed at the end of this set of exercises (see page 140).

   c) If the level drops significantly, repeat the exercise and add substance to it (example: "I am stuck and feel pressured...")

   d) *Note: the level of disturbance may never drop to zero. The aim of this exercise is to lower the level to a point where you feel capable of doing constructive action aimed at resolving the issue*

7) Pause for a moment and explore this statement: "If I were not doing [what keeps you from doing better], what would I be doing?"

Covering one eye during the process is crucial to gaining access to hidden information you need from your non-dominant brain hemisphere. The "not nots" tend to tease the mind with possibilities and confuse the dominant brain hemisphere. The "I am" statement tends to focus attention on the issue at hand while simultaneously addressing the strongest and most powerful logic level - identity.

Some possible variations

Some Common Thinking Errors and What to Do About Them

1) Before covering one eye with the palm of your hand, picture yourself doing what you want to do, the way you sabotage yourself, or whatever you are doing that keeps you from peak performance. Notice how the image changes as you proceed with the process.

2) While you are doing the statements, blink your eyes a few times.

3) Instead of (or perhaps in addition to) covering your eye, do the following eye movements:

   a) While looking far to the left, say statement 1 - I am...

   b) While looking far to the right, say statement 2 - I am not...

   c) While looking far left again, say statement 3 - I am not not...

   d) Reverse the order - starting with looking far right and saying statement 1 - I am...

   e) Same as the previous idea with the eyes traveling up and down (vertically) or diagonally instead of horizontally. Remember to always reverse the order of the movement/statement so as to capture as much information as you can.

Dual Hemisphere Technique

A technique for goal-oriented outcomes

Hypnotherapy and NLP are superbly suited to goal-oriented outcome therapy. Often, however, the client relapses or has difficulty getting "in state" and the therapy seems to come off less than spectacular – the client may even complain that s/he did not accomplish what s/he wanted to accomplish with the therapy.

It could be that the therapy you invoked did not address the hemispheres of their brain in such a way as to maximize the therapy. In NLP we learn that each person uses their senses to access their experience of their world. The most popular of those senses being sight (visual), sound (auditory), and touch (kinesthetic). What we don't spend much time on is hemisphericity or addressing each hemisphere differently than the other.

In the human brain there are two distinct hemispheres in the cortex. That means we have two distinct individuals living in our heads – each preferring different modes and experiencing and interpreting sensual input differently. In addition to the two hemispheres of the cortex we also have an emotional center called the limbic system and a primal brain known as the reptilian brain that sits below the limbic system. Each of these centers of brain activity interprets sensual input differently.

Basically, the reptilian brain interprets according to a strict rule of survival – it is always asking, "Is this a threat or a treat?" The reptile has only two concerns – 1) to avoid pain; 2) to seek pleasure. That's it – all based on survival. Anything perceived as painful or potentially painful is automatically avoided or escaped. Anything perceived as pleasurable or potentially pleasurable is sought. How it avoids potential pain (threat) is with historical fight or flight strategies – automatically invoked and carried out.

The limbic system's job is to communicate between the reptile and the "human" cortex. When the body feels something, the limbic system translates that feeling into something the cortex can identify – like an emotion. Actually, all emotion we can identify and acknowledge is really our cortex trying to make sense of impulses from the body. We call it anger – the body calls it racing heart, flushed face, clenched fist, and tight jaw. The human brain then sets about making sense of the impulses

Some Common Thinking Errors and What to Do About Them

– coming up with a reason for the condition – "she made me mad when she said I was worthless."

The cortex is divided right down the center – right and left. You might think of the right side like the guy in a helicopter looking down at a train – seeing the entire train, where it came from and where it is going. The left side might be thought of like the guy standing next to the tracks watching each car go by one at a time – s/he sees each car closely and can inspect minute details.

One hemisphere is dominant over the other at any given time – they are never dually dominant. We would go crazy and confusion would reign if we could experience duality simultaneously. We naturally switch dominance about every two or three hours – unless a specific task is required of us that keeps one dominant a little longer. Repeated tasks tend to make us favor one hemisphere over the other over time – eventually making one hemisphere dominant every time we do a certain task. The problem there is that we never get to view it any other way – we get stuck in a task/hemisphere rut.

We can voluntarily switch dominance – the crux of the dual hemisphere technique. Most people are probably quite unaware that one hemisphere is dominating a given moment's experience. We think we are using our whole brain all the time and never give hemisphericity a second thought. Certainly both hemispheres are working all the time – brain scans bare this out. Nevertheless, one is dominant over the other so far as our awareness is concerned – we are unaware that we are mostly using one input. We are unaware that there is "another way to look at this."

The technique is simple and straightforward. Whatever you are concerned about right now – in a session this could mean when a client is faced with a fear or a setback – realize that you are looking at it in one of two ways (at least). Then, cover one eye with your hand and consider the problem again. Did it change? If not, cover the other eye and reconsider the problem. Did it change?

Another way to do this is to imagine your "problem" out in front of you. "Look" at it with both eyes open. Then cover one eye and look at it again. Did it change? Cover the other eye – did it change again? Elicit insights gained from each hemisphere by asking for insights while each eye is covered. Explore what happens.

Some Common Thinking Errors and What to Do About Them

Each brain hemisphere holds vital information about the issue. While one is active it automatically jumps to the fore and makes itself dominant – subjecting the other to obscurity. To activate the other brain hemisphere – and gain the information available there - all one has to do is activate it by causing it to become dominant. This can be accomplished quite simply by covering an eye, thus shutting off the input to one hemisphere and causing the other to become more dominant – usually enough so to become dominant.

So, which eye is dominant for you right now? It's easy to check. Just square your body to an item at least 20 feet away and point at the item with either hand (righties will tend to use their right hand and lefties their left). With both eyes open, point directly at the item. Now close your left eye and see if the pointing finger moved. If it did move, you are dominant in your right brain hemisphere at that time. If your finger remained over the item, you are dominant in your left brain hemisphere.

Like NLP sensual representational modes, most people tend to favor dominance in one hemisphere over the other – that is, spending more time dominant in one hemisphere than the other. Intentionally switching between each side can balance the hemispheres and bring useful information into awareness for consideration – usually resulting in a solution to a problem or issue.

Some Common Thinking Errors and What to Do About Them

Eye Patching (Pirate Therapy)

A simple technique for change

If you continue to see life as you have always seen it, you will tend to get more of the same as you have gotten in the past. Sometimes you must take drastic steps in order to make a change. Sometimes you must change the way you see life to affect a change in your life. Some people spend much of their time unconscious of what is going on around them because when they are dominant in one hemisphere that hemisphere is shut down – maybe as a normal condition.

A simple little item like an eye patch – one that covers the eye while it is open – can make a shut down hemisphere come back to life. You might see it like a husband and wife who have a serious communication problem. He thinks he's right all the time and wants to make sure his wife is, too. So, he imposes his will upon her and makes her behave the way she should. This is like the two hemispheres – the left (masculine) can overwhelm the right or vise versa, causing one hemisphere to shut down nearly completely – even though it has useful information. It just doesn't express itself because it is used to being put down or ignored.

Here's the drill. Place an eye patch over one eye for a few minutes – 5 or so – no longer. Then place the patch over the other eye for the same amount of time. Notice how you feel – physically, emotionally, and mentally during the time your eye is patched. Do this every day for a week. Then increase the amount of time you patch your eyes. Increase the time you are patched to 30 minutes gradually over 6 weeks. This should awaken any submissive or dismissed hemispheric information. That means you will probably come up with novel ideas, solutions, considerations, and answers. You may even make a real change in your life!

If you feel sick or queasy, take off the eye patch - you have just gained important information from a hemisphere that is used to being shut down. Rather than not patching, patch for shorter periods of time until you can wear the patch without feeling sick.

Remember – while the patch is on your eye you no longer have depth perception so:

- Do not use sharp implements like knives while you are patched.

Some Common Thinking Errors and What to Do About Them

- Do not drive or operate dangerous equipment while patched.

- Do not traverse a stairs or walk where you need depth perception while you are patched.

- Do have conversations with others while patched.

- Do read while patched – you will most likely substantially increase your reading speed.

- Do watch TV while patched – you may notice a change in preferences in programming or you may gain insights you were unaware of before – or, you may notice that after watching half an hour of TV, you don't recall a bit of it!

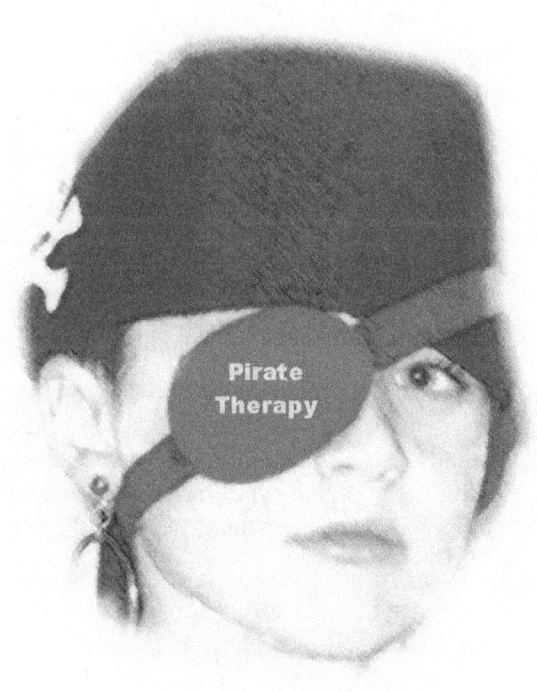

Some Common Thinking Errors and What to Do About Them

THE Exercise for Manifesting Conscious Desires

A gift of power to you that you have always owned... ...and maybe forgotten...

I know – every purveyor of change has an exercise that will magically change the world for you. And they all claim their exercise is the best and ultimate – especially if they want you to buy it!

Well, I'm offering this one free of charge (okay, you purchased this book, so it's not entirely free of charge). The only cost to you is your time, which if you will invest in yourself, will pay immeasurable dividends. I've shared this exercise before and some have even "tried" it. If today is the day you say "I'm making a change in my life NOW," then now is the time to actually do this exercise – do it every day several times a day for the rest of your life!

Some people take pills every day – without fail. Maybe you are one of them – or maybe you take a vitamin supplement every day just to ensure proper body chemistry and optimize your physical well-being. If that is the case, then you know how easy it can be to make a daily habit out of doing something simple and quick.

I'm leading up to this exercise because I want you to get a sense of how easy yet powerful this one exercise is. It's not a secret or magic elixir – although I would categorize it as magical and mystical. There is nothing for you to buy or prepare – no gym shoes or sweats to buy or get out of mothballs, although most of us could use a little more aerobic exercise...

Because the exercise is simple and easy to do, you may feel that it can't possibly do what I say it will do. The only way to find out for yourself is to do the exercise every day for 6 months – give it a real good test. After 6 months of doing the exercise every day, set a time for you to take notice of what is and has been happening in your life. Notice changes and why they changed.

To prepare you for the exercise I'm going to describe an exercise I did with a Life Skills class a few years ago. We were discussing the principle of Thought – that thought brings about manifestation in the physical. I suggested that we could move a chair in the room with nothing more than our thought. We chose a chair and where we would move it to – its orientation in the room and all. Once we were all agreed upon the result

Some Common Thinking Errors and What to Do About Them

of our thought, I simply got up, went over to the chair, picked it up, and moved it to the location we had previously agreed upon.

"That's silly," you might say to yourself. "He moved it physically rather than with his thought – he cheated." And you'd be completely right – and wrong! What caused the muscles in my body to move my body to the chair, lift the chair, and move it to another location? The magic of thought did that. For those people other than me who were simply thinking about the chair moving – they got their wish – the chair moved without them touching it in any way but with their thoughts. The instrumentation of the movement (my body getting up and physically moving the chair) was insignificant compared to the fact that the chair moved with only thought. The whole concept is amazingly powerful and, to those who "get it," life-changing in the positive.

Taking responsibility for life is the key to conscious manifestation. You will manifest life whether or not you are aware of it. Taking charge of your life is merely a matter of taking note of it. We usually get tossed by the winds of life because we do not realize that it is we who are doing the blowing!

Alright. Enough preparation. Here is the exercise. Do it every day as often as you can remember to do it and at least once a day for the rest of your life – or the next 6 months anyway:

1. Notice things around you and what they are doing (sitting on the desk, making a noise, moving up and down, stopped at a stop sign, etc.)

2. Tell those things around you to do or be what they are currently doing or being (tell the car to be stopped at the stop sign just as it is doing now, for example)

3. That's it! Do this to as many items, people, and circumstances as you can in a few seconds (like 30 seconds to a minute – longer if you have time). You can even do this as a sort of mental gymnastics while sitting in a meeting or walking to work or talking with someone.

The important thing about this exercise is to DO IT! Do it often. Within a very short period of time you will begin to notice that you can "foretell" happenings. At first it will seem to you that you are foretelling the future of events – some have told me they thought they were developing their intuitive powers. Later you will understand that things are happening BECAUSE you are in charge of those happenings and things. You are in command.

I've used this simple exercise with clients who report feeling depressed, anxious, and in pain. In every case where the client has actually done the exercise daily they have dramatically reduced or eliminated their stress within a very few days.

Remember – this is not about guilt or blame – it's about responsibility and power. Responsibility you already have and maybe have felt you could abrogate by blaming others, circumstances, or yourself. Interestingly enough, too, once a person realizes that s/he is in charge of the dimension, their perception of the dimension changes radically – they find themselves in a position of power and tremendous influence and wanting to do positive things with that power – they are at conscious choice, a condition few of us actually get to experience in this life.

And that makes all the difference.

You might ask, "If this is such a powerful exercise, why isn't everyone doing it?" The answer is, "They are!" They just aren't aware of it. You, too, are doing this very exercise every day – you fully accept your perception as true and act accordingly.

Perhaps we might take a moment to investigate the power of acceptance and action.

Some Common Thinking Errors and What to Do About Them

Acting Accordingly

Consider for a moment why you have what you currently have and why it is that things are the way they are. You accept things that way and act accordingly.

For example, you accept that trees are green and rain is wet. You do not question nature as it is - you simply accept it. Perhaps EVERYTHING in your life is as it is because you accept it that way - and act accordingly. When was the last time you questioned something in your life that you take for granted - like air? Over time, you have come to simply accept things as they are - for the most part; you take your life for granted.

Your education level is what it is; your spousal situation is what it is; your income is what it is; your personal health is what it is; the world situation is what it is; etc. You accept it by observation. That is, you observe the way things are and that's that - you trust your senses to give you an accurate picture. And you accept your picture and act upon the picture accordingly.

You become "happy" with the way things are and tend to keep things as they are with your acceptance of them – along with appropriate action.

Even in times of what seems like massive change in one's life - like divorce, for example - MOST of your life is as it has always been. Your attitudes are pretty much the same, trees are still green in the summer; telephone service still works like it did; you still sweat when you exercise; you still breathe air; blood flows through your body as it did before. Very little is actually changing.

Where life is different, is where you notice it as being different. The rest remains the same - just as you have accepted it and are now acting accordingly. That means that even the largest changes you want in your life are actually miniscule compared with everything else in your life.

And here is the secret to life change - IT'S EASY. Very little actual energy must be diverted to make substantial change. The reason change seems hard is because we have ACCEPTED life change as difficult and act accordingly.

Here's how easy it is - accept something as true and act accordingly - and that is the new way things are.

Some Common Thinking Errors and What to Do About Them

To prepare for a life change, one can use a well-known technique called pretending. Until you actually accept a new way in life, you can pretend first - it's like a half-way method. However, once you ACCEPT that things are a certain way AND act accordingly, things will tend to remain as they were - because that is what you actually accept and act upon accordingly.

Want to make a change? Accept something ELSE as true and ACT ACCORDINGLY.

To make a real change in life, all you must do is no longer accept things as they were - in other words, accept the new to the exclusion of the old. You are so used to doing this, you probably no longer notice it when you do it. When you choose to take the bus instead of the car, for example, you are accepting one way to the exclusion of another. When you choose to take a shower instead of a bath, you are accepting one way and no longer accepting the other. This happens so often in the course of a day that you may not notice how often you do it - how often you choose, accept and act accordingly.

The very first step in manifesting what you want is to notice that YOU ALREADY HAVE WHAT YOU have accepted and you act accordingly. If you don't like some aspect of your life today, it's not anyone's fault - it is merely a consequence of your acceptance of what you believe your life to be - and you've acted accordingly - making it manifest in that manner.

Choose again – and act accordingly.

You may have to pretend until you believe.

Some Common Thinking Errors and What to Do About Them

Taking Action!

Ah, New Year's Day. Many of us like to make New Year resolutions - expressing ways in which we would like to see our lives change for the better. Maybe this will be the year we quit smoking, or take up golf, or lose that weight. Whatever it is we want to change, our first action is to NAME the change we want to make. We have done this part so often that we now take it for granted - meaning we have become oblivious to it.

You are already taking action on what it is you really want - it's automatic - you do it unconsciously. Based on your beliefs, you take action that is appropriate with what you accept as true - your beliefs. You don't even have to think about or plan anything – you're already doing it - automatically. It might help, though, if you were to recognize that you are already taking action.

Why, then, do you not get what you want? The truth is - you DO get whatever it is you want. You just don't recognize it - because you are so used to accepting what you get from life. And based on what you accept, you tend to act accordingly, reinforcing your belief that what you accept as true is, indeed, true.

If you continue to act as you have acted in the past - you will continue to get what you have always gotten in the past. If you continue to believe as you have believed in the past you will continue to get what you have gotten in the past – because you will tend to act accordingly!

There are really only two ways to change what you get from life:

1. Change your beliefs about whatever it is you want.

2. Change your actions based on your beliefs about whatever it is you want.

The reason you don't have what you think you want is because you don't realize that you already have exactly what it is you want. It's called feedback - if you want to know the meaning of your communication with the universe, check your feedback. If you want to know what it is that you really want in life, check your life feedback.

Changing your beliefs is a matter of disassociating cause from effect. If you are poor because you don't make enough money, you have a cause-effect relationship built between being poor and not having enough money. You may have fortified this belief with substantial amounts of evidence - but all that evidence is based on the same premise - the SAME BELIEF - the same cause-effect relationship.

Break your cause-effect relationship and you break the belief. Break the belief and you set up the possibility of a NEW BELIEF - one based on a new cause-effect relationship. It's so easy - and you already know how to do it - it's your human nature to create cause-effect relationships at will.

To change your actions, simply change your cause-effect relationships (beliefs) and the action will flow like water from a spring - with virtually NO EFFORT on your part.

Okay - the secret to making new cause-effect relationships...

Perception!

Here's a simple exercise you can practice that I guarantee will break up old cause-effect relationships and open doors to making new ones.

Remember - this is easy! You do it all the time so you've grown accustomed to it and maybe take it for granted. So, when we do it with AWARENESS, things get interesting.

1. Mantra #1 - "I could be wrong about this." Say it as many times as you can every day. As long as you believe you are right, you will continue to justify your past behavior and strengthen those old cause-effect relationships into the future. Further, you'll do your best to defend your rightness.

2. Realization - "Everything I perceive is feedback for ME." - couple this step with the previous one. Your perception could be wrong! Accept it. Remember - YOU are not wrong - it is your perceptions we are challenging.

3. Mantra #2 - "I now have exactly what I most want." This fortifies your responsibility for creating your life - and helps strengthen the fact that you are experiencing feedback. Couple this step with the first step - you could be wrong about this as well. You have only what you perceive that you have. And your perception could be so wrong!

Some Common Thinking Errors and What to Do About Them

4. Mantra #3 - "When I change my perception - EVERYTHING changes to support my new perception."

Based on the above 4 steps, we ask the following questions:

1. In what ways could I be wrong about this?

2. In what ways could what I'm experiencing be feedback for me?

3. In what ways could I be getting exactly what I really want?

4. In what ways could I perceive this differently?

Okay, now let's put this little exercise in mantra building into a practical example - losing weight.

In 2003, I conducted a weight management course for a few people who were clinically obese. Each dropped weight and kept losing weight at the rate of about 2-4 lbs per month. And the weight has stayed off. During the 5-week, 2-hours per week, course, we challenged our cause-effect relationships.

Here are some cause-effect relationships we challenged during the course of our class:

-   "Every time I even think about eating desert I gain weight."

-   "Every time I lose weight I just gain it right back plus some."

-   "Every time I try to lose weight, I fail."

-   "If I lose weight and look really sexy, men will try to rape me."

-   "If I lose weight and look sexy, nobody will take me seriously. They'll judge me according to my looks instead of by my personality."

-   "I've always been large." (so, I'll always be large)

Each of us created our own mantras based on the above 4 step example - and created our own questions to ask ourselves at each point. The questions in particular are valuable because they tend to stir the brain to work with you - to act.

If you never question something it will tend to continue as it is.

Some Common Thinking Errors and What to Do About Them

QUESTION YOUR BELIEFS!

One woman questioned her beliefs about her weight like this:

1. In what ways could I be wrong about eating and weight gain? (this is a setup for release of old cause-effect relationships)

2. In what ways could my being obese be feedback for me? (this is a question of identity - "who am I?" - setting the mind up for a new identity based on a new cause-effect relationship)

3. In what ways could being obese be exactly what I want right now? (this sets up change - big time - as it puts into proper perspective the relationship between cause and effect - and who is responsible for the change)

4. In what ways could I perceive my body shape differently? (this sets up imagination of the actual shape of the change - and measurement of it when it occurs)

Of course, you will have to do some specific activities to release the weight - like eating well and exercising. It's just that when your old cause-effect relationships are changed and you are sliding down hill instead of trying to fight your way up the hill, eating properly and exercising will come NATURALLY and EASILY - as though they were automatic. You will find suddenly that the foods that used to pack on the pounds may suddenly take on a foul taste; or the exercise you were doing suddenly becomes more fun (or maybe somebody shows up in your life to make that exercise easier and more motivational); or perhaps you'll get "ill" and drop some weight (this is often a simple body cleanse and is normal in a good weight management course of action).

In weight management it is imperative to let go of HOW your body transforms and stay focused on your compelling image of WHAT you want.

You can apply the above concepts to any endeavor - any resolution.

You may also want to consider simply breaking old cause-effect relationships and experience what happens next - without any direction at all from your mind. This would require some bravery on your part as it means giving up all claim to rightness - what I might consider abject humility and the loss of pride - although there is really nothing to lose because you never really had anything of substance anyway - all you had was a perception. You would also have to release any defense of any kind. When you don't have to be right you also do not need to defend yourself. It may mean taking on vulnerability as a way of life.

Change without mind direction requires total courage - the kind of courage seldom seen and yet admired and loved when encountered. You have that kind of courage. I know this because you are still here - you have survived – against the odds! Against tremendous odds, you were born. Through darkness and troubles in your life - you persevered. Through your own self-imposed prisons you have come this far. Amazing! How did you do it? How did you become so courageous as to even consider making a permanent life change?

Cause-effect relationship #1 - because you have come this far in life, you can achieve ANYTHING - poverty or riches, heavy or light, health or illness, whatever you truly wanted you have achieved.

Some Common Thinking Errors and What to Do About Them

Simple Weight Management

As long as you consider your weight/body image situation as permanent or long term, it will be. In order to make your body more responsive to a body image change - quicker - you must release your need for it to take a long time to change. Further, releasing your need to have the process be difficult or nearly impossible will help as well.

Let's start by releasing the need to make change hard, difficult, or impossible to do. Amazingly, this can be as simple as a statement made with full congruency (defined as when body, mind, and voice are in alignment). Here's what you do - while nodding your head in agreement, say to yourself, "I suppose that it IS POSSIBLE for me to weigh [weight goal or desire] in a matter of [time goal] weeks." Remember, that your statement MUST be doable - telling yourself that you will weigh 100 lbs by this time next month when you weigh 200 lbs now is ridiculous and your body knows it. So, be realistic, yet challenge yourself.

Telling yourself that IT IS POSSIBLE to achieve can eliminate a lot of your resistance and make it much easier to do. Remember - you will NEVER achieve what you believe to be impossible. Those who have achieved the "impossible" did it in believable steps - one at a time. "By the yard it is hard - by the inch it's a cinch." It may very well be impossible for you to achieve a 100 lb body on a 200 lb frame - to say the least of how dangerous it would be as well. It would not be impossible to weigh 160 on that same 200 lb frame. THEN the 160 pound body could then look into the possibility of weighing 150; then maybe 140; and maybe even 130 - over time.

To get things kicked off toward gaining control of your body weight, let's investigate your current mindset. When you wake up in the morning and put your body before the bathroom mirror, are you surprised to see your body in the mirror? Or, are you resigned? Does the image you see look "normal" for you? That is, do you simply accept what you see in the mirror as "the way you are?"

Some Common Thinking Errors and What to Do About Them

Have you grown accustomed to your body image? Do you have a set of emotions that accompany that image? Disgust? Anger? Resentment? Helplessness? Hopelessness? Sadness? Overwhelm?

That is what I call your mindset - as it relates to your body weight and image. Boxed up together, your mental image and your emotional feelings about your weight comprise your current mindset. EVERYTHING you think, say, do, or feel, are filtered through that mindset. You act like a person of your weight/body size - for example, you wear large or tight clothes; you see big numbers on the scale when you stand on it; you feel heavy in your body; you hear other people call you fat; you may even feel that others exclude you from their activities; think you are ugly, not good enough, or defective. Mindset!

You see, it's not your body's fault that you weigh what you weigh and look as you do. It's your mindset! You have set your mind (in concrete). Let's start by breaking up the concrete!!

Here's a fun exercise I've used successfully to break up mindsets about weight:

When you stand before a mirror first thing in the morning, look at the image with absolute shock – as though you were genuinely surprised to see your body at its current size. In your mind you play a little game:

- "ACK! What happened to my body through the night?!!"

- "Just last night my body looked [describe the way you want it to look]"

- "It looks so DIFFERENT now!" (it can help to point out those areas where you "notice" the difference the most)

- "This must be some kind of temporary condition, like a cold (because I was just fine last night when I went to bed), and I'll soon be back to normal..." (put this in your own words to suit yourself. IMPORTANT – make sure you compare your body size

Some Common Thinking Errors and What to Do About Them

condition to some kind of condition you have previously overcome in a short time – like a cold or flu)

If your weight truly were a temporary condition like a cold or fever blister (or temporary weight gain), you'd be concerned but not devastated or resigned. Instead, you'd probably see your doctor, take some medicine or whatever and see to the problem right away – so you can be okay the next morning.

I wonder what would happen over a couple weeks if every morning you did this little exercise. Of course you'd have to vary it a little each day so your natural inclination to normalize would not simply make it an empty ritual – for example, you might look in the mirror one day with less shock and say to yourself, "I can hardly wait to be over this temporary condition." Or, "It looks like I'm getting better – it won't be long now…" Or, "Damn! It looks worse today than yesterday. Oh, well, colds are like that, too – sometimes it gets worse before it gets better. And I will get better soon…" Or, "Hey, look! The swelling has gone down some on my thighs. Soon all the swelling will be gone and I'll be back to normal."

In addition, if you told yourself that eating [a healthy diet] and doing [some kind of exercise] will cure the temporary condition, you might be more motivated to do it and see faster results. You can enhance this, too, if you can convince yourself that a CERTAIN food or pill or activity IS THE CURE for your temporary weight gain, you can eat that food, pill or do that activity and associate it with a weight drop. This is best done AFTER you notice some success - simply attribute your success to something you eat or do. One woman I worked with noticed a weight drop and told herself that the weight drop was due to the chocolate she had eaten the night before – she dropped almost 20 lbs in just two months eating chocolate!

I think you get the idea – if I think of my excess body weight as a "temporary condition" it's a lot easier to manage than if I think of it as an insurmountable problem that I've had all my life… …and that seems to be getting worse over time... ...and no matter what I do I keep gaining... ...hopeless, helpless, overwhelmed... blah, blah, blah......... you get the picture.

Some Common Thinking Errors and What to Do About Them

Hemispheric Motivation to Achieve Goals

Mathias Pessiglione, of the Brain & Spine Institute in Paris, and his colleagues showed[14] that motivation could be subconscious - and can be associated with brain hemispheres. Apparently, you can be more motivated toward a goal if you face that goal with your most motivated side. Now THAT is some useful information!

Suppose you find yourself setting a goal but having difficulty achieving it. Maybe the reason is not environmental (i.e., you don't make enough money), or internal in the way you might suppose (you're not worthy or smart or good enough, etc.). Suppose the problem with non-achievement has to do with which way you physically turn your body in relation to "where" you represent your goal achievement to be in space.

For example, suppose you make a goal to slim down this year. So, you go about setting up a series of short term sub-goals to help you work your way up to achieving your longer range goal of having the body you want. Maybe you follow a goal achievement program and write your goal and sub-goals down. But at the end of the goal time frame, work as you may, your goal seems just as distant as when you started.

This time, instead of writing it all down, maybe posting your goal on your fridge, etc., you get a photo of your desired outcome - that new healthy body (remember, this is an example - your goal could be much more esoteric) - and post it to your fridge. This time, though, you turn your body to the left - your head, too - so that you see your photo to the right side. NOW, check inside and rate your level of commitment to that goal (maybe on a scale of 1-100). Next, move your body in such a way that your photo is to the left of your visual field and again check your level of commitment to the goal (on the same scale). Which side has the higher number?

Every time you gaze at your photo on your fridge, make sure your body is in the very same position as it was for the higher level of commitment (motivation). Even avoid looking at the photo from the other side. Let the motivated side help you achieve your goal.

It also occurs to me that your other, less motivated side has resources the more motivated side needs in order for you to achieve your goal. Let those resources come to you by moving your eyes horizontally, vertically, diagonally, and zigzag up to down to up - rather than looking in the less motivated direction at your photo.

Because your motivations are subconscious, just let the exercise of moving your eyes do the trick of sharing resources - rather than TRYING to make those resources available or WORKING to find them. Instead, you might be able to simply face your goal - on one side, that is...

The Illusive Commodity

Of course you know what you are thinking about right now. Maybe you are thinking about your lunch or the kids or a project you are engaged in. Or maybe you are totally focused on my words right here as you read them. The ability to focus on one train of thought to the exclusion of others is the illusive commodity of which I write.

It's called a scotoma - a thought that blinds you to other thoughts you may be having simultaneously to this one. You are always employing a kind of scotoma. That is, you are focusing on one or two trains of thought to the exclusion of others you are having simultaneously. If you entertained every thought simultaneously, you'd go mad in a hurry. Why? Because you are always in the mode of action upon thought. Every thought in one direction is simultaneously thought of in the opposite direction - just not acted upon as much.

Your mind tends to vacillate between opposing thought trains - thinking in one direction then the opposite then back again - in microseconds. It's like thinking in yes-no-yes-no... all the time. What gets you anywhere and why you achieve action on anything is that you spend just a microsecond longer in one direction than you do in the other - that is, you spend more time in the yes direction, for example, than in the no direction.

That means it is unnecessary to focus 100% of your energy into a single thought train in order to achieve results. In fact, it is impossible to focus 100% of your thought energy into only one thought train - because you are always in possession of the opposing thought train simultaneously.

Rather, to achieve a goal only requires that you shift your gaze - your attention - in one direction MORE than in other directions. For example, in order to tie your shoes, you only had to focus maybe .01% of your total thought energy to the task - the rest of the thoughts were probably scattered fairly evenly among a hundred other thought trains.

Your mind is not an all or nothing affair. It is capable of and engaged in multiple thought trains in hundreds if not thousands or more directions. And it is considering all these things simultaneously. Attention, however, is the ability of the mind to attend to one thing and attenuate all others - like picking out a voice in the midst of a noisy room. In this case, you would not need to have the room absolutely quiet in order to understand the words. All you would need is sufficient difference from the background noise to make out and understand the words s/he is saying. While you are viewing this computer screen, you are also seeing everything else in your field of view simultaneously - why you are not overwhelmed is that you are attending to this one task and attenuating in importance all others. We sometimes refer to this ability as paying attention.

In order to achieve a goal, all you have to do is place just a little more attention upon your goal than upon the background noise of other things - other thoughts - that vie for your attention. Pain is a wonderful example of how one thought can be attended to while others fade in importance. If you've ever had a pain somewhere and suddenly get hurt more in another place on your body, you know that the shift of attention can "cure" the original pain. That shift of attention was perhaps as little as 1% of your total thought processes going on at that time - but it was sufficient for you to feel and believe that you had total focus on just that one thing.

What I am suggesting here is that you are always in balance - always at null - nonexistence. What makes you believe that you exist and have volition and thought and experience - is an amazing and illusory condition called attention. This wondrous ability to shift our enormous thought energy in one direction or another presents us with the illusion of experience, the illusion of physicality, the illusion of volition or free will.

A system that is in total balance would, for every action, create an equal and opposite reaction (Newton's first law). If I extend out 5 units in one direction, I am also simultaneously extending out in the opposite direction the same 5 units. What makes it seem like I'm moving in any direction is that I'm attending to (focusing attention on) one direction while neglecting the opposite. The truth is that I have not moved at all, but the effective experience is that I've moved 5 units in one direction.

I'm a pretty practical guy and this stuff starts to sound more like fiction than science of any kind. So, let me bring this down into something practical, usable, and pragmatic for you. Let's say that you'd like to drop 20 pounds by a certain time and keep it off forever. Further, that you'd like to strengthen your body so that it looks good when it weighs 20 pounds less than it does now. These are good, perhaps achievable goals - and let's pretend for this discussion that the goal is yours.

You already have a focus and attention that provides you with an experience of a body the way it is now. To redirect your thoughts and experience in the direction of a body 20 pounds lighter does not require a 90 degree turn - or even a major lifestyle change - rather it only requires a slight shift or nudge to one side or the other - in the direction of your goal. A tiny nudge every day is every bit as effective as a major lifestyle change - but a whole lot easier to sustain over time.

To make a "shift" rather than a turn sets the mind up for "it's easy" to achieve my goal - because I don't have to do anything major to achieve it - just shift my thoughts rather than change my mind or reorganize my whole belief system. Can you feel the difference between having to make a major life change and simply making a slight shift? If all you had to do was lean a little toward the left rather than push or shove or pull hard to the left, wouldn't it seem easier to achieve?

As long as you believe that you have to make BIG changes, you will fight and struggle to achieve your goal. As long as you believe it is easily achievable, however, you will make it. When you believe that your goal is easy - as easy as tying your shoes, for example - you will achieve it quickly and easily - just as you believe.

Remember - a simple step to one side changes everything.

Some Common Thinking Errors and What to Do About Them

Letting Go Of Outcome

When I say "let go of outcome" I mean, "Just let what happens happen." Don't concern yourself so much with the HOW - the METHOD – focus instead on the WHAT – a compelling image of what you want.

I've seen people actually thwart their own success by dictating to their bodies how the weight loss should occur ("ooh, I've lost 10 lbs this week! That's way too fast – I better start eating better [more]"). Even my doctor does not really know what my body is capable of doing for me – so when I dictate to my body HOW it should release weight, I can get in my own way. So, letting go of the outcome means I release my attachment to HOW I get there. I still want to hold solidly to my compelling outcome image – the WHAT of the equation.

Somewhere within us all is a "knowing" of what and how much we should eat and how much we should exercise to maintain optimum health and vitality. When the compelling image of what you want to look and feel like is sufficiently motivating, your body will automatically prefer foods and exercises that will support achieving that image.

Finally, when releasing the HOW, I place my trust in my body to do what it needs to do to achieve my compelling image. IF the compelling image is appropriate for my body, it will work itself hard to achieve it – and will ultimately succeed if I (my mind) stay out of the way. IF that image is not appropriate for my body, it will still work itself hard to achieve it yet might come up short. That is good feedback for me that I have chosen an inappropriate body image for me – it's a cinch that at 6'3" tall and 54 years of age, I do not want to weigh in at 120 lbs – it's inappropriate for my body and it knows that and will only go so far with that image – maybe even nixing it right off the bat. IF my compelling image is strong enough, however, my body will achieve that 120 lbs – yet I may not like the results (emaciated looking, scrawny for my body height, insufficient muscle mass to sustain activities, much more susceptible to disease, etc).

If your body is accustomed to being heavy – like that's the way you have always been – it's very unlikely that your body will suddenly feel "right" about being thin (although it could). It might take some getting used to – like chunking down slowly. For example, a 400 lb woman in one of my classes dropped to 380 for a while – then to 360 for a while –

Some Common Thinking Errors and What to Do About Them

then all the way to 350 for a while. It's been over 9 months now and she is still at just under 350. That is marvelous for her body. Once her body is used to 350 for a while, it might agree to drop down even more – we'll see. At any rate, we did not tell her body HOW to do this – it just did.

To get your compelling image set into your body - like a revamped blueprint - let's do a simple, yet powerful visual exercise.

- Stand in a room where you have some room in front of you - maybe 5-10 feet in front of you.

- Imagine your "perfect" body image in front of you. Place it like a hologram in a physical location in front of you. If it feels like the image should be off to one side or the other, that's okay - unless the image is off so far that you can't see it - then just bring it back and place it firmly in front of you - pin it to the carpet if you have to.

- Cover one eye and describe this perfect body image - in as positive language as you can - while looking at your perfect image - look right at it while you speak out loud. If negative "buts" come up, imagine placing them into a bucket or box right beside you (doesn't matter which side). Pay particular attention to how your body feels - sensations, etc. - just notice.

- Cover the other eye and describe your perfect body image - again in as positive language as you can - while looking at your perfect image - again looking directly at the image there in front of you. Again, place any "buts" into the bucket or box beside you. Pay particular attention to how your body feels - sensations, etc. - just notice.

- Get a sense of the feelings you'd have IF you had that perfect body RIGHT NOW. How good would it feel to have someone you like say, "Damn! Girl! You look really great! What have you been doing?!" How would it feel to be able to easily: climb that mountain; hike that trail; run that marathon; play that game; dance all night; love yourself? Put all that information into the image in front of you.

- MAKE THE IMAGE COMPELLING!!!

Some Common Thinking Errors and What to Do About Them

- Now - the magic - go stand in the space where you placed your compelling image. See through the eyes of your compelling image; hear through the ears of your compelling image; feel what it feels like to be in your compelling image's body. EXPERIENCE IT! Take your time - enjoy the sensations.

- Get a sense of the feelings you're having IN that perfect body RIGHT NOW. How good it feels to have someone you like say, "Damn! Girl! You look really great! What have you been doing?!" How good it feels to be able to easily: climb that mountain; hike that trail; run that marathon; play that game; dance all night; love yourself!

- Now look back at where you were standing. Cover one eye and notice how your body feels - looking back at itself the way it WAS. Cover the other eye and notice again - just noticing and acknowledging.

- Now - bring this image with you as you step back into the area where you were when you started this exercise. Bring all the feelings, sensations, knowingness of what it is like to BE that image - bring it all back with you.

- Standing in your original position on the floor, turn around and with your eyes closed, imagine BEING your compelling image IN THIS SPACE. Allow whatever body sensations to express themselves - just let it be. Open your eyes and notice any differences in body, mind, eyesight (do things look brighter, for example), ideas, sounds, inner voice, emotions, etc.

- You are now your compelling image - rather, your compelling image is "imprinted" into your body. It's time to let go of outcome as I described above.

Some Common Thinking Errors and What to Do About Them

Using Chemistry

Do you recall the last time you got angry with someone? Or sad about a situation? Or frustrated when things went "wrong?"

How long did it take you to "cool off?" A few minutes? An hour or more? A day? Never?

Would you like to be able to instantly cool off and get your brain back under control? You can do it with this simple process.

First, you must realize that you are feeling a negative emotion. Like when you notice your voice volume rising for no reason - like being in a noisy room. Or, maybe your face feels flushed with embarrassment.

As soon as you notice your physical or emotional condition, quickly ask yourself the following question:

"Could I be experiencing a temporary chemical imbalance right now?"

Notice then how quickly you cool down.

Why does this work so well?

- You are asking a question which breaks the mind state you created already. Your mind goes into "search for an answer" mode which is different than the "you are to blame" mode.

- You assign possible "blame" to someone or something else than what you had previously assigned.

- You give your brain something ELSE to work on - temporarily distracting it and getting it to work on balancing your brain chemicals instead of focusing in on and sustaining the present condition.

Chemicals in the body are responsible for a huge array of behaviors. When chemicals get out of balance, the whole body system goes into active behavior the mind believes will reestablish equilibrium.

For example, note what happens to people who become inebriated. Their behavior often changes from their norm - it's the body's way of seeking equilibrium. Would you blame the negative behavior of a drunken person on the alcohol or on them personally? Usually people say it's the alcohol talking. That's chemistry.

Some Common Thinking Errors and What to Do About Them

When you question your motives - looking elsewhere for "blame" than what you originally thought - magic happens.

Try it and see what happens to you.

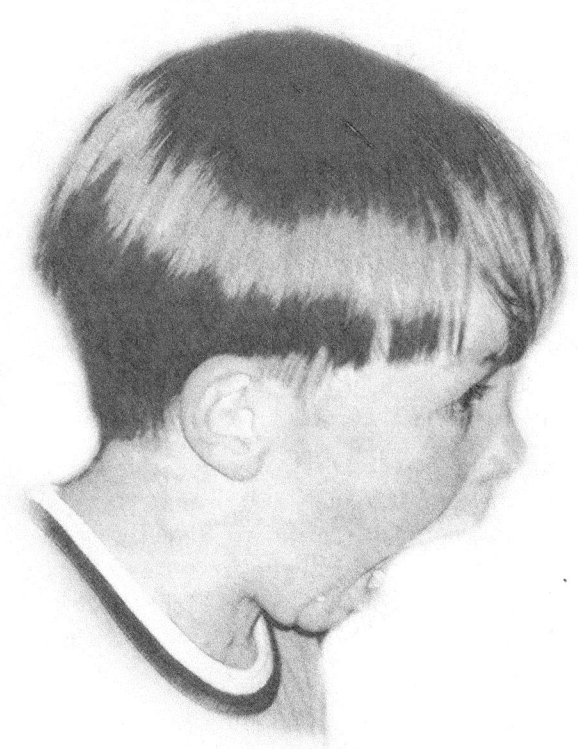

Identity or Chemistry?

Some Common Thinking Errors and What to Do About Them

1-Minute Excuse Buster

Are you plagued by excuses? Maybe you want to get something done but your "excuse builder" builds a nice little excuse for getting you out of whatever it is. Sometimes, we excuse ourselves from doing what we really want to do with excuses that range from time constraints, to money constraints, to relationship constraints.

It's all bogus! No matter how valid the excuse, if it's an excuse, it's an excuse! And you know it!

Would you like to beat an excuse right NOW? - Like in the MOMENT it comes up? Well, you can. And it's easier than you may think.

The next time you want to do something but find yourself blocked by an excuse - for example, "I'd ask my boss for that raise, but I just don't have the time right now..." or "I'd quit smoking right now, but I just bought a brand new carton yesterday and I don't want to waste money..." or "I'd go back to college and get that degree but I'm too old to start over again..." - BUT, BUT, BUT...

1. Speak your excuse out loud to yourself. Do your best to state it with a "but" in the sentence - like, "I'd do it, but..." (the basic structure for an excuse)

2. Evaluate just how valid the excuse seems to you - on a scale of 0 - 10 with 10 be absolutely 100% valid. By valid, I mean that the excuse is not really an excuse. Rather, it is a valid reason - like, "I can't go skiing with you this weekend because I will be out of the state visiting my parents..." Do you sense the difference here. A rating of 10 means it is not an excuse at all. Okay?

3. Now notice how your body feels when you speak your excuse out loud to yourself. SPEAK OUT LOUD each body sensation - "I sense a twitch in my left eyelid..." - get specific and downright honest with yourself here. EVERY sensation must be accounted for - so be thorough.

4. Now once again, speak your excuse out loud and measure its validity. You may find that the validity of it has dropped to zero and you feel empowered to go and do what you had previously excused yourself from doing.

Some Common Thinking Errors and What to Do About Them

Now, to give yourself some energy to go and do what you want to do, you must engage your most compelling state of mind. Here's how you do that:

1. State what you want to do out loud with conviction: "I AM going back to school next term." Say it with conviction - meaning a commitment to yourself that you WILL do what you say you will do - COMMIT. If you find yourself promising and later reneging, you are excusing yourself - repeat the 1-minute excuse buster above.

2. Notice how your body feels. Account for every sensation and movement.

3. Speak out loud EVERY sensation and movement. For example, "My right hand jerked."

4. Repeat the entire process until no body sensations and/or movements occur.

5. You are now in your most compelling frame of mind for THAT issue.

When your body and mind are together on a project, it will get done - because you have created a compelling state of mind and body. Like sliding down the slide, you will find yourself achieving your objective with far less effort on your part.

To add some extra energy, you could do an energy circle about your new commitment:

1. Stand upright.

2. Draw a circle with your mind - right in front of you - where you will be standing in just a moment.

3. State your "I AM" statements concerning your commitment - "I AM going back to school NEXT TERM!" "I AM calling the registration office TODAY!" "I AM getting my finances in order TODAY!" "I AM calling my counselor TODAY!" - Say these OUT LOUD to yourself.

4. Imagine placing EACH statement into the circle.

5. If you notice any body sensations or movements, state them out loud - "My left eyelid is twitching". This time body sensations

Some Common Thinking Errors and What to Do About Them

are part of your commitment - so acknowledging them simply strengthens your resolve.

6. Once you have all your statements of commitment in the circle, step into the circle with PURPOSE and COMMITMENT. Step into the energy of those statements.

7. Imagine those statements sinking into your anatomy - into your body. This is more than simply putting them on like clothing - breathe them into every cell of your body - and imagine your body cooperating and accepting all your statements.

8. Go about your day. Notice how things seem to fall into place for you...

The Lucky Mind Game

How hard must you work to make a significant life change? Must you "bust your buns?" Maybe you have to "really get down to it." Or perhaps you feel that you must hit "rock bottom" first. What is your belief about making significant change in your life? How hard must you work to get what you want?

The Western work ethic has influenced me and many like me for centuries - perhaps millennia. Basically stated, one must work for one's keep. Work is good. Hard work is better. Working hard to achieve what you want makes it somehow worth more.

Further, we tend to judge richer people as harder workers and better people than poorer people - not that we believe it is true in every instance - only that we tend to believe it to be true generally - based on an old cultural bias - our work ethic.

What does it take to become wealthy? What does it take to become happy? What does it take to become smarter, better looking, wiser, quicker, better.

Working harder is not necessarily the answer! Working smarter is not necessarily the answer! - although both are great and useful models for some.

Why is it that one person wins the job, raise, sale, prize, or contest when there are so many fully qualified applicants? The fact is, raises don't always go to the most qualified or worthy; contests are not always won by the best qualified applicant; the sale doesn't always go to the best product or sales presentation.

Occasionally, after giving your best effort, fulfilling all the requirements, and exercising your most positive attitudes and thoughts, the prize goes to someone else. Does that mean you are somehow not worthy? Does it mean you didn't do something right or work hard enough at something you should have in order to gain your goal?

Perhaps J. Paul Getty, one of the most successful oil barons of all time, wrapped it up best when he said, "Rise early. Work hard. Strike oil."

Let's look at that statement again.

"Rise early." Get enthusiastic! Can't wait to get started!

Some Common Thinking Errors and What to Do About Them

"Work hard." Dig in and do what must be done - ACT.

"Strike oil." Get lucky!

So, what does it take to be "lucky?" What work can one do to make one lucky? The answer is - NONE. It takes no work at all to be lucky. It just takes luck - that's all. And no amount of work can replace good old-fashioned luck!

You can, however, improve the odds that you will become lucky. For example, J. Paul Getty was lucky he struck oil. And he improved the odds that he would find oil by using the proper methods to find oil, hired good people to do the explorations, and was ready with a plan when the oil came in. Like he said - he rose up early, worked hard, and THEN struck oil (got lucky).

You may not wish to strike oil. However, when it comes to achieving that long wished-for goal, you might find luck a useful friend. To increase the odds of you encountering some luck, you must put yourself in a lucky frame of mind.

A lucky state of mind is - receptive! That means giving yourself the OPTION to feel okay about receiving something without working hard to get it. If, for example, someone GAVE you a significant amount of money - a gift - would you feel that you owed them something for giving you the gift? If so, it is not a gift but a loan or debt to be repaid. You would also be guilty of theft - by stealing their gift - turning it into a debt instead. You would NOT be receptive!

EVERY DAY, someone gives you a gift of some kind - the electric company supplies you with electricity, the sun shines on your world, air fills your lungs, someone shares a smile with you. So many gifts!

Must you repay them or owe them a favor? If you feel that you must repay or owe them, you put yourself in a different position than receptive. Now you are in a contract - a mortgage situation in which you are indebted - you are now NEEDY - needing to repay the debt. Luck tends to avoid the needy - just check the statistics on lottery winners - very few are needy.

Gratitude is the garden in which luck grows and flowers. When you FREELY GIVE and RECEIVE energy - without strings - you open the floodgates of your own LUCK channel.

Some Common Thinking Errors and What to Do About Them

To keep it all in perspective - enthusiasm without hard work and luck is great but takes you nowhere. Hard work without "luck" and some enthusiasm is just hard work with no place to go. Luck without enthusiasm and hard work is boring and goes nowhere. Gratitude builds enthusiasm, action, and luck.

The Lucky Mind Game

For 7 days, in ONE area of your life, GIVE freely - no strings or expectations. This is a mind thing only. You must not change anything that you currently do - just change the inner thoughts about what you are doing when you do it. Instead of paying a bill, for example, think of it as giving a gift to that company - because you want to (after all, don't you normally give to people you want to give to?).

When you receive something - a smile, a kind word, a compliment, money, etc., accept it graciously as the gift it was meant to be - with a silent "thank you" - FREELY - without any sense of needing to pay it back or having any obligation attached to the gift. Just receive it - that's all.

If you receive a bill in the mail, treat it as a gift - a reminder for you to stay with your mind game - when you pay the bill - and WITH ENTHUSIASM (rise early), pay the bill as soon as you can (work hard).

Notice what happens to you after one week - 7 days. Just see if the Lucky Mind Game helps you achieve your goals just a little easier.

Keep up the Lucky Mind Game for a month... a year... for the rest of your life. The Lucky Mind Game is one way of turning gratitude to your advantage - applying it in a positive way. Enjoy.

Some Common Thinking Errors and What to Do About Them

It's All In Your Head – So Use It!

Feeling low on confidence? Wish you were prettier, more handsome, or more attractive? Wish you could stand in front of an audience and speak with confidence?

Maybe it's time to stop wishing and start BEING!

Sounds like some kind of advertising hype doesn't it? Well, with a simple technique, you can actually do all these things and much more. You'll be amazed at how simple yet profound this little thought process is. Give it a good trial for at least 30 days and you will no doubt notice a more confident, beautiful, attractive you.

Before describing the simple exercise, I'm going to discuss briefly why it works so well.

To begin with, you are not seeing these words on the page. Most certainly not. You are not feeling the book in your hand either. You are not hearing the sounds in the room you are in. Rather, you are experiencing electro-chemical impulses within your brain that you interpret as real things in your experiential dimension.

Further, those things you experience are not really there except as you interpret them. In other words, it's all in your head – your interpretation.

This same thing applies to everyone - not just you. Everyone is making interpretations of their sensual experiences.

Now for the power part - those others who experience you are not really there! You are imagining them - interpreting your experience of their experience. It's all in you. You are the one who perceives what others perceive. You do this by thought - the kind of thought that comes from belief. What you believe IS.

When you believe that you are ugly, you tend to seek out evidence to make your belief more real – to sustain your belief. Therefore, you tend to taint the perceptions of others about you by placing in their minds the thought that you are ugly - because their minds are just your interpretation of your belief about you imposed upon your belief about who they are. It sounds very confusing - which tends to keep you unaware.

Let me illustrate from my very favorite movie of all time, The Matrix, wherein a young boy is bending spoons and Neo, the protagonist, asks the boy how he could bend spoons -

(boy) "Do not try and bend the spoon. That's impossible. Instead, only try and realize the truth."

(Neo) "What truth?"

(boy) "There is no spoon."

(Neo) "There is no spoon?"

(boy) "Then you will see that it is not the spoon that bends. It is only yourself."

Neo goes on to not only bend spoons but become "the one" - the ruler of this dimension. You are already there - the ruler of your dimension of perception and thought - you're just unaware of it!

Finally, here's the technique:

- Pretend that everyone you see, hear, or feel, is experiencing you as beautiful, confident, loving, attractive, or any other way you would want to be experienced by others.

That's it!

What you are doing is predisposing them to perceive you in the way you want. Further, you'll tend to act accordingly, reinforcing your perception of their perception of you - call it mind control. Actually, what you are doing is minding your own mind.

Some Common Thinking Errors and What to Do About Them

The Power of Pretending

One of the things psychology has determined is that good mental health includes a modicum of control over one's life. When your life feels out of control, your mental health will quickly deteriorate. When you feel in control of your life, you feels secure, happy, and usually enthusiastic and healthy.

Pretend for a moment that you are in total control of your life. Pretend that you are suddenly aware that this "life" is nothing more than a dream in which you have forgotten that you have another "life" in another state - the state of awakened consciousness. Maybe you can pretend that your "real" body is lying asleep on a couch or bed somewhere.

Pretend that you are suspicious about your experience of life - that maybe it's not what it appears to be.

If you were to become suddenly aware that your "real" body was sleeping elsewhere and that your life as you know it now was really a dream, what would you do?

- What would you DO?

- What WOULD you do?

- WHAT would you do?

If you were to become suddenly aware that your "real" body was sleeping elsewhere and that your "life" as you know it now was really a dream, how would you feel?

- HOW would you feel?

- How WOULD you feel?

- How would you FEEL?

If you were to become suddenly aware that your "real" body was sleeping elsewhere and that your "life" as you know it now was really a dream, who would you be?

- Who would you BE?

- Who WOULD you be?

- WHO would you be?

Look around you right now and pretend that what you are experiencing is a dream and that you can control it by merely thinking - as you would if you suddenly became aware that you were in a dream. Pretend that you could bend the dream to your will. Imagine how that would feel.

Imagine doing, feeling, and being what you want to do, feel, and be in your pretend dream. Infuse the feeling into every dimension of your being - feel it, see it, hear it, taste it, smell it, BE IT.

Now, get up and walk to a place where you can extend your arms fully out beside you. Extend your arms and spin around in a circle slowly for three full turns. Stop spinning and place your hands on your knees or thighs and breathe in deeply and out easily and say, "YES!"

Notice how you feel. Notice how much better you feel about your life. I believe you will notice a pleasant difference.

Some Common Thinking Errors and What to Do About Them

That Reminds Me

Quickly sharpen up your memory

Here's a quick exercise to get your brain and memory working faster and more efficiently. It's basically an acknowledgment of the way the human brain works. Exercise makes the brain stronger, faster, and work longer.

Start with a simple observation – any will do. Maybe look out the window and say, "My, what a sunny day it is today!" Keep it simple.

Next, append to that observation with a memory, "That reminds me of the time…" – linking a meaningful memory to the observation you just made. For example, after saying the statement in the previous paragraph, you might append with, "This sunny day reminds me of the time we went fishing at Fishermen's Bend and I caught that big steelhead salmon…"

Next, append to your last statement in the same way you just did. For example, "Steelhead fishing at Fishermen's Bend reminds me of the time we went out of Newport and the boat engine died and we had to row back in…"

Keep going with, "…and that reminds me of the time…"

Don't worry about whether or not the linked memory makes sense in the context of the previous linked memory, just speak it anyway and keep going. Speak your statements out loud to yourself or someone you trust. I like the idea of speaking out loud to yourself – it keeps others off balance about you.

Do the exercise for as long as you wish. To exercise your mind and brain cells, you only need to do this exercise for 5 minutes or so a day. Within a month you should see dramatic improvement in memory and recall skills.

All for One and One for All

What if you are using your thoughts to justify who you believe yourself to be. And that to that end, you project your self-perceptions upon others. Some examples might include seeing your own trust embodied in a trusted leader; maybe you embody your own affections in a friend or relative you believe is affectionate; or you embody your own confidence in an authority figure. All these are ways in which you might project yourself out onto others.

Perhaps you've heard the saying, "You can only see in others what you have within yourself."

When you change whatever that is within you, others change. It's that simple - and you are doing it all the time. You change - the world changes. When the world changes, it indicates that you have changed.

It would appear, however, that you are not in charge of your own thoughts - merely the processor and justifier of those thoughts that flow through from "on high."

I propose that you begin now to take back the charge of your thoughts. Instead of reacting and justifying you must become proactive.

You and I have been trained since we were babes to think in a certain way. Especially in the West we expect explanations in order to make things work for us. You are reading my explanation right now - maybe even enjoying it - BECAUSE it titillates your inherent justification mechanism.

Now the shocker - if you are to take charge of your thoughts, you must STOP THINKING IN THE WAY YOU HAVE BEEN THINKING IN THE PAST. You must GIVE UP JUSTIFICATION. That means ditching the word "because" altogether.

The word "because" is the word most used to join effect to cause - what happened (effect) with why we did it (cause) - justification. It is just plain backward to thought flow. You've confused cause with effect - turning it all backwards. Neuroscience is just now demonstrating how well we do it - at least in the Western world.

How can you turn around your thinking?

Some Common Thinking Errors and What to Do About Them

First - you must do something about your becauses. A really good therapist will ask you for your justifications - your becauses - by asking such things as, "...and you feel that way because..." - eliciting your justifications - which holds your backwards thinking process in place.

As you address and release your becauses - your justifications - you find that you need them less and less. At some time, you may even find that you can play with them just a little. For example, you may play with the concept that you believe yourself to be such and such a way because there is a bird on the lawn in the back yard. This "nonsense" turns reason on its ear!

Next - listen to how many times you use the word "because." Does it flow out of your mouth without so much as a quiver? Are you so adept at its use that you feel that you have mastery of it? Are you a Doctor of Justification (a DJ)? How addicted are you to your justifications? Must you always be right, justified, or at least proper? Listen to yourself and others - count how many times you hear the word, "because." Muse over this.

Then - take positive action. Here is the drill:

- Sense things as they are - see the green grass, hear the birds, feel the chair under your buttocks.

- Tell those things to be as they are. Tell the grass to be green, the birds to sing, the chair to support your buttocks. Do this to EVERYTHING you perceive. EVERYTHING.

- Give it absolutely NO FURTHER THOUGHT.

Do this drill every day for a month - longer if you want to really "go for it."

Soon you may notice such things as you being able to "predict" an event before it happens - telling a car to turn a certain direction or a person to say something in advance of it happening. If you will not get lost in the amazement - keep doing the drill - you may experience something few have experienced in this dimension of becauses. I'll leave this open for your experience - if you choose to pursue it.

I wonder what lies beyond justification and reactive thought.

Just Because

Some Common Thinking Errors and What to Do About Them

Years ago, I was posted to guard a flag pole outside the post headquarters. I guarded it all night as I was ordered. In the morning upon being relieved of duty, I inquired about the flag pole guarding duty. My immediate superior just repeated, "because we were ordered to guard the flag pole." I got this same answer from each of my superiors as I went to each of them one at a time climbing the chain of command - until I got to the post commander, who repeated the same slogan.

In desperation, I turned to the post historian. In the post records he found that at one time, shortly after the post was built, the flag pole was set in concrete and a guard was posted to keep people from disturbing the hardening concrete. The order was never rescinded and had carried on for almost a century until someone came forward and questioned it.

After that, the flag pole stood on its own without a guard posted to protect it.

Some Common Thinking Errors and What to Do About Them

Pirate Therapy - Simple and Powerful

Eye patching - sometimes referred to as "Pirate Therapy" has been in my therapeutic tool bag for some time. And as a whole therapy model, it is fantastic - and easy. To do eye patching, simply purchase a good eye patch - one that allows one to keep the eye open while it is patched, and use the patch as often as you can.

Let me show you a simple, yet powerful technique you can use on yourself and others to jump start change - assisting you and them in achieving therapeutic goals quicker and with a whole lot less effort. You can do this process on yourself - although I recommend doing it with someone else.

"Pirate Therapy"

1. Choose a therapeutic goal - what life will be like when you have what you want and are being the way you want to be - or you have solved your problems - maybe what you will be like when you are completely healed and whole.

2. Sitting or standing, facing straight in front of you, get a sense of where the image of you in your "clear" state would be - maybe it's off a little to the right or left - just get a sense of where in front of you that image feels "right." Point to it while remaining in a squared body stance looking straight ahead of you. If the image insists on being directly in front of you, choose to put it to one side or the other - it doesn't matter which side, so long as you move the image to one side - then point to it while remaining body squared to the front. Call this image your compelling image.

3. Imagine putting the image of you in your current condition to the other side off center as far as you did with the other image. Call this your resource image.

4. Keeping your head and body squared to the front - looking straight ahead - move your eyes to the resource image and look directly in that direction while holding the head still facing directly forward. Your eyes should now be off center in the direction of your resource image.

Some Common Thinking Errors and What to Do About Them

5. Cover one eye with your hand or place an eye patch over one eye - either eye. Continue looking in the direction of your resource image while keeping both eyes open with one covered. NOTICE ANY AND ALL SENSATIONS IN YOUR BODY.

6. Move the cover to the other eye and repeat the previous step.

7. Now direct the eyes in the directions of the compelling image - the image of what and who you want to become. Remember to keep the head and body squared to the front - move only the eyes.

8. Cover one eye with your hand or place an eye patch over one eye - either eye. Continue looking in the direction of your compelling image while keeping both eyes open with one covered. NOTICE ANY AND ALL SENSATIONS IN YOUR BODY.

9. Again switch the cover to the other eye and repeat the previous step.

10. Now imagine merging the two images right in the middle - directly in front of you. Just wait until this feels complete. You might use your arms in front of you in a sweeping joining movement. This is the merged image.

11. Cover one eye with your hand or place an eye patch over one eye - either eye. Continue looking in the direction of your merged image while keeping both eyes open with one covered. NOTICE ANY AND ALL SENSATIONS IN YOUR BODY.

12. Move the cover to the other eye and repeat the previous step.

For many people, this little exercise opens internal resources that will now be available during sessions. Even if you are doing this for yourself, the resources suddenly available may be enough to resolve presenting issues right in the moment.

Some Common Thinking Errors and What to Do About Them

Success Formula

"If A equals success, then the formula is:

$$A = X + Y + Z$$

X is work. Y is play. Z is keep your mouth shut."

- Albert Einstein

Question: "What would you do if money were no object and you were assured of success?"

Juice is the stuff of manifestation.

You are always creating what you most love by focusing your attention upon it. The trouble most of us have is that we are unaware that we are creating what we most want every second of every day. What's more, we are setting ourselves up to enjoy even more by ruminating, worrying, and fretting. All that attention makes the juices flow - the juices of fear.

Juice is the stuff of manifestation.

We are human, with physical bodies, so we can experience physicality. Physicality means experiencing sensations. When we have certain combinations of physical sensations, we call it emotion. Due to cultural and family conditioning, we associate mental constructs with physical sensation and call it an emotion. Anxiety, for example, is a complicated combination of physical sensations coupled with mental constructs (I feel anxious because...). Emotion is not real without a physical component - "emotion" without physical sensation is simply a mental construct we've called an emotion.

In the world of manifestation, we combine our thoughts into solid experience by focusing attention. Most of the time we focus that attention upon combinations of physical sensations and mental constructs - what a busy life we lead inside our human bodies! Usually our physical bodies and mental constructs hold our attention pretty well. So well, in fact, that we become oblivious to what we are really focusing our attention upon. Juice follows attention. Action follows juice. Manifestation follows action.

It's all about the juice!

Some Common Thinking Errors and What to Do About Them

Sometimes we need a little help so that we can get out of our own way. Einstein alluded to it in his quote. Keeping one's mouth shut is equivalent to getting out of one's own way. To do that, we stop talking about our troubles and the "whys" behind our inaction or non-success, and begin to direct our speech toward acknowledgement of the facts - that we already have what we most want in life.

And that's the big secret behind success in any endeavor - acknowledgement that we already have what we most want. To assist you (and me) in this concept, I've developed a little game that played daily will develop in you monumental power to direct your life and help you gain success in whatever direction you please.

It's quite a simple game. A game you may think is too easy. You see, it flies in the face of traditional thinking that says if you work hard enough you will be successful at something. It also flies in the face of the goal-oriented Great American Way. You may have to suspend all your beliefs about how to succeed for a while so you can play this little game.

Are you ready? I hope so, because I can't wait any longer - my curiosity is at critical levels! TELL ME NOW!!!

I hope you felt your blood pressure rise a little while your curiosity rose to this occasion. You see - it's in the juice that manifestation finds itself - it's all in the juice.

Okay, here's the game. You must play it every day at least once a day for 30 days to master the game and begin to take charge of your manifestations - mind what you want because you WILL get it.

1. Go back to the first question I asked you at the beginning of this section. "What would you do if money were no object and you were assured of success?"

2. Ask yourself the question.

3. Then SHUT UP! For as long as you can, think nothing. Let your mind just go blank.

4. Count to 15 out loud.

5. Then say to yourself: "I now have exactly what I most want."

If you wish you can also close with a "thank you" or "amen" or whatever suits your fancy.

Some Common Thinking Errors and What to Do About Them

That's it.

Just imagine what you could do!

Some Common Thinking Errors and What to Do About Them

Getting Out of Your Own Way

Sometimes I get in my own way. I think I know what I want to do, yet I find myself thwarting my own efforts - self sabotage. What's more, I find myself judging myself for all that sabotage saying, "It's my fault. I didn't do what I was supposed to do to make this work." blah, blah, blah. Sound familiar?

If you, too, sometimes sabotage your own efforts, the answer to the problem is almost sickeningly easy – just get out of your own way!

Okay, now you ask, "And how do I do that?"

That's a mighty good question, and one to which you already have the answer. Don't you just hate it when someone tells you that?

What you don't have is the key or conscious awareness of that answer. Perhaps you will find it in this exercise. That is my intent and hope for you.

This simple little writing exercise might bring about awareness and assist you in finding the key to getting out of your own way. Write the part in *italic* and fill in the part in brackets [ ]:

- *The ways I sabotaged myself today (or yesterday) are:* [nice long list] Example: "I stayed in bed today and missed a golden opportunity to call a prospective client - thereby losing a client and keeping my practice small."

- *The choices I made that brought about the ways I sabotaged myself today (or yesterday) are:* [get creative here - what was I thinking? what were my unconscious choices based upon the results I experienced? - that kind of thing] Example: "I chose to stay in bed longer because I feel afraid to call."

- *The feelings I chose in myself as a result of the sabotage are:* [list them all - down and dirty] Example: "I choose to feel afraid." "I choose to feel not good enough." "I choose to feel lazy." etc.

- Now the kicker - look at your lists and say to yourself out loud, "I am choosing to experience these things and feel this way about it."

Some Common Thinking Errors and What to Do About Them

To get out of your own way, you must simply become aware that you are the cause and the effect. This is not a blame game. This is an accountability game. When I get it that I am both cause and effect, I can then make a new, conscious choice, and then, with fearlessness, enjoy the journey.

I am Cause and I am Effect

Some Common Thinking Errors and What to Do About Them

Get an Attitude

Everybody deserves to have at least one person in their life who is totally, completely, wonderfully in love with them. Someone who realizes how magnificently awesome they are.... Someone who understands their unique beauty and one-of-a-kind personality....Yes, someone whose heart thrills at the sight of them and whose eyes light up and say "OH. WOW! YOU ARE SO GREAT!"

I call it, understandably, the "OH WOW attitude." Babies need to have this attitude expressed to them many, many times in order for them to pick up the message that they are wonderful, worthwhile human beings. With repetition, they will begin to make it a part of themselves.

How does this apply to me as an adult?

It has been found that humans need to hear 3 times more positive things to balance out each negative they perceive. And the omission of a positive is felt as a negative. Contrary to popular belief, it is not possible to overdo it in this department.

When you express an OH WOW attitude to your baby or child, you are investing in their self-esteem, an essential building block for their future happiness. When you express an OH WOW attitude to yourself, you are investing in your own self-esteem and your own overall health. It is better than money in the bank! So don't be afraid to let it show.

So, here's a little exercise you can do that can have amazing results over time.

Look into a mirror at your face and look yourself right in the eye and pretend that you are looking onto the eyes of the one you love the most. Pretend that the person you are looking at "through the mirror" is your soul mate, your perfect love. Then, out loud, say, "Oh, wow!"

The ancient Sufi writer, Rumi, knew of the power of this exercise when he penned his poetry over 7 centuries ago. He wrote about himself (and me):

"You come to us from another world - from beyond the stars and the void of space. Pure. Of unimaginable beauty. You are the essence of love. You transform all who are touched by you. Mundane concerns, troubles, and sorrows dissolve in your presence bringing joy to ruler and

ruled. You bewilder us with your grace. All evils transform into goodness. You are the master alchemist. Light the fire of love in earth and sky, in heart and soul of every being. Through your loving, existence and non-existence merge. All opposites unite. All that is profane becomes sacred again."

Translated by Coleman Barks and featured in the 2 CD set, "A Gift of Love" by Deepak Chopra and Friends.

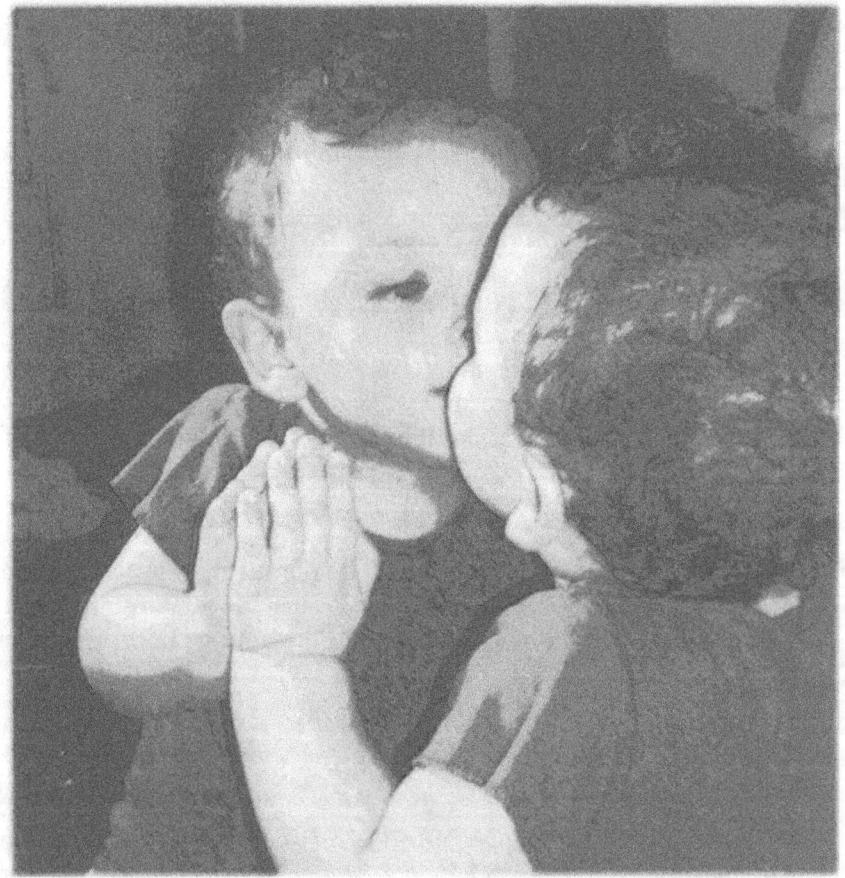

Everybody deserves to have at least one person in their life who is totally, completely, wonderfully in love with them. Even babies know who best to love.

Some Common Thinking Errors and What to Do About Them

What to Do About Self-Judgments

It's said that Tom Watson, one-time head of IBM, was asked if he was going to fire an executive whose recent mistake cost the company six hundred thousand dollars. Watson shook his head and explained, "I just spent six hundred thousand dollars training him. Why would I want anyone else to hire his experience?"

Actions we might call mistakes are often the learning we need to make that next big life move. Sometimes we get really wrapped up in guilt about our "mistakes" when, by doing so, we miss golden opportunities for real mindful and meaningful change in our lives.

I wonder what would happen if you were to view your "errors" and "mistakes" as "education" and "experiential learning"? Would it make a difference in how you went about achieving something with that education?

Changes are usually easier to make when one starts with the premise that they have the education and experience necessary to make the changes. When you are seeking to achieve a certain job or position, do you not first attain the necessary education and experience to qualify for the job? You certainly don't judge that education and experience as bad or wrong, do you? So why place that kind of judgment on other kinds of education or experience?

Sometimes we unconsciously say judgmental words about ourselves that reveal how we view ourselves in our world. If, for example, I judge myself to be confused, I might also apply to the word "confused" a whole system of values, feelings, and beliefs that I lump together into "confused." By saying, "I'm so confused," I'm actually saying (without saying it) that I am experiencing a plethora of emotions, values and beliefs that I have created to support my definition of "confused."

Because I accept that my definition is the correct definition, and, to a very large extent, the ONLY correct definition (especially for me), I find myself unaware of alternatives that might also work for me – without all the "baggage." Instead of thinking of myself as being confused, for example, I might consider using "curious" or "inconclusive" instead - giving me the air of inquisitiveness rather than defectiveness.

Some Common Thinking Errors and What to Do About Them

To give you some ideas in this area, I've included a list of expressions on the next page.

Whenever you hear yourself say one of the words in the left column, quickly switch it over to one in the right column. It will work better if you use your own list of reframed expressions. Just make a list of your most commonly used self-judgmental words and phrases. Then counter each phrase with a similar word or phrase that puts a new light on the subject while keeping the general concept intact. The whole idea, again, is to get you off your default definitions and on to something more useful to you.

With practice, the whole thing will become automatic – to the point where you will automatically think of reframes before you speak them. In time, the old definitions will be gone along with their emotional and judgmental cargo.

Negative Expression:	Transforms Into:
• Confused	• Curious
• Depressed	• Not on top of it
• Destroyed	• Set back
• Disgusted	• Surprised
• Embarrassed	• Stimulated
• Exhausted	• Recharging
• Failure	• Feedback
• Humiliated	• Uncomfortable
• Impatient	• Anticipating
• Insulted	• Misunderstood
• Irritated	• Stimulated
• Lonely	• Temporarily on my own
• Lost	• Searching
• Overloaded	• Stretching
• Overwhelmed	• In demand
• Rejected	• Under-appreciated
• Sick	• Cleansing
• Stressed	• Busy, Energized
• Stupid	• Learning
• Terrible	• Different

Some Common Thinking Errors and What to Do About Them

On the other hand, we could just change our definitions. After all, the English language is replete with ambiguity. Sometimes how a word sounds is funnier than its dictionary meaning. Here are a few examples:

- Arbitrator \ar'-bi-tray-ter\: A cook that leaves Arby's to work at McDonald's

- Avoidable \uh-voy'-duh-buhl\: What a bullfighter tries to do

- Baloney \buh-lo'-nee\: Where some hemlines fall

- Burglarize \bur'-gler-ize\: What a crook sees with

- Control \kon-trol'\: A short, ugly inmate

- Eclipse \i-klips'\: what an online barber does for a living

- Eyedropper \i'-drop-ur\: a clumsy ophthalmologist

- Misty \mis'-tee\: How golfers create divots

- Paradox \par'-uh-doks\: two physicians

- Pharmacist \farm'-uh-sist\: a helper on the farm

- Polarize \po'-lur-ize\: what penguins see with

- Primate \pri'-mat\: how to remove your spouse from in front of the TV

- Relief \ree-leef'\: what trees do in the spring

- Rubberneck \rub'-er-nek\: what you do to relax your wife

- Seamstress \seem'-stres\: describes 250 pounds in a size six

- Selfish \sel'-fish\: what the owner of a seafood store does

- Subdued \sub-dood'\: the kind of, like, cool boat that, like, runs underwater, man

- Sudafed \sood'-a-fed\: to bring litigation against the USA's central bank

It doesn't always have to be so serious, you know…

Some Common Thinking Errors and What to Do About Them

Resources

Joseph Bennette, MRET, CHt
www.JosephBennette.com
www.Powerstates.com

The Rapid Eye Institute
Home of Rapid Eye Technology
www.rapideyetechnology.com
503-399-1181

Emotional Freedom Technique
Gary Craig
www.emofree.com

Oregon Hypnotherapy Association
www.hypnosis-oregon.com

About the Author

Joseph Bennette has trained thousands of people in Rapid Eye Technology, Emotional Freedom Technique, Hypnotherapy, and Life Skills. He has been a featured presenter at Northwest Hypnotherapy Conferences, Oregon Hypnotherapy Association meetings, on radio, television, and community events.

Until retiring in 2007, Joseph had an active hypnotherapy practice specializing in anxiety and anxiety-related emotions like panic, irrational fear, worry, fretting, and destructive self-doubt.

Joseph Bennette was trained in Rapid Eye Technology at the Rapid Eye Institute, Salem, Oregon, and holds a Master level certificate. He completed courses of study in hypnotherapy at the American Institute of Hypnotherapy, Santa Ana, California, and American Pacific University, Honolulu, Hawaii. He is also trained in Neuro-Linguistic Programming (NLP), Parts Therapy, Group Leadership, and Communication Technology. He is certified as a Clinical Hypnotherapist and is a member of the Oregon Hypnotherapy Association.

Joseph is the author of several books, numerous articles in trade publications, and is a frequent contributor to several online forums and email groups.

If one only wished to be happy, this could be easily accomplished; but we wish to be happier than other people, and this is always
difficult, for we believe others to be happier than they are.
Charles De Montesquieu

Some Common Thinking Errors and What to Do About Them

Endnotes

---

[1] John A. Ball, The Zoo Hypothesis, Elsevier Science, 1973.

[2] Adapted from *Biocentrism: How Life and Consciousness Are the Keys to Understanding the True Nature of the Universe*, by Robert Lanza with Bob Berman, published by BenBella Books in May 2009.

[3] So says Maurizio Corbetta, M.D., the Norman J. Stupp Professor of Neurology at Washington University School of Medicine in St. Louis, MO. (Tosoni A, Galati G, Romani GL, Corbetta M. Sensory-motor mechanisms in human parietal cortex underlie arbitrary visual decisions. Nature Neuroscience, 2009.)

[4] Thomas and Lleras' article in Psychonomic Bulletin & Review is titled *"Swinging Into Thought: Directed Movement Guides Insight in Problem Solving."*

[5] Study source: University of California, San Diego. Coauthors on the study are Paula Niedenthal and Nathalie Dalle, both at the Universite Blaise Pascall, Clermont-Ferrand, France.

[6] Sources:

Captive Hearts: Captive Minds, by Madeleine Tobias and Janja Lalich, Hunter House, 1994; pgs 101-103

Take Back Your Life Recovering from Cults and Abusive Relationships, by Janja Lalich and Madeleine Tobias

Feeling Good: The New Mood Therapy, David Burns, M.D.

Unlimited Power: The New Science of Personal Achievement, by Anthony Robbins, Joseph McClendon

Encyclopedia of Systemic Neuro-Linguistic Programming and NLP New Coding, by Robert Dilts & Judith DeLozier

[7] This Meta Program was identified by L. Michael Hall and Bob Bodenhamer who describe it as follows: "Whether a person first looks at the problems, dangers, threats, difficulties, challenges of a situation or the opportunities, possibilities, wonders, excitements, and thrill determines whether their mind goes first to worst- or best-case scenarios. Sorting for the best-case scenario orients one in an optimistic, hopeful, goal-oriented, and empowered way. Sorting for the worst-case scenario orients one in a pessimistic, negative, and problem-focused way." -- *Figuring Out People*, 1997.

Some Common Thinking Errors and What to Do About Them

[8] Karl Szpunar, lead author of a study on the relationship between memory and future thought and a psychology doctoral student in Arts & Sciences at Washington University.

[9] Robin J. Tanner (Duke University), Rosellina Ferraro (University of Maryland), Tanya L. Chartrand (Duke University), James R. Bettman (Duke University), and Rick Van Baaren (University of Amsterdam)

[10] The Other Mind's Eye, Allen C. Sargent, Success Design Intl Publications, September 1, 1999. ISBN-10: 0967483107, ISBN-13: 978-0967483108.

11 *When learning and remembering compete: A functional MRI study.* Huijbers W, Pennartz CM, Cabeza R, Daselaar SM (2009) PLoS Biol 7(1): e1000011. doi:10.1371/journal.pbio.1000011

[12] A neuro-linguistic programming term for the process by which memory recall, state change or other responses become associated with (anchored to) some stimulus.

[13] LiveScience.com April 25, 2007
(www.livescience.com/humanbiology/070425_eyes_memory.html)

[14] Psychological Science, a journal of the Association for Psychological Science

www.ingramcontent.com/pod-product-compliance
Lightning Source LLC
Chambersburg PA
CBHW060334290526
45793CB00003B/618